PRAYER

PRAYER

THE GREAT MEANS
OF OBTAINING SALVATION
AND ALL THE GRACES
WHICH WE DESIRE OF GOD

Saint

ALPHONSUS LIGUORI

SCOTTS VALLEY
CALIFORNIA
2010

Prayer: The Great Means of Obtaining Salvation
and All the Graces Which We Desire of God

Saint Alphonsus Liguori (1696–1787)
(Alfonso Maria de' Liguori)

Edited by Eugene Grimm

This paper is acid free and meets all ANSI standards for archival quality paper.

Typeset in Minion Medium 11 / 15

ISBN 9781450546539

To the Incarnate Word,

Jesus Christ,

the Beloved of the Eternal Father.
the Blessed of the Lord,
the Author of life,
the King of glory,
the Savior of the world,
the Expected of nations,
the Desire of the eternal hills,
the Bread of heaven,
the Judge of all,
the Mediator between God and man,
the Master of virtues,
the Lamb without spot,
the Man of sorrows,
the Eternal Priest and Victim of love,
the Home of sinners,
the Fountain of graces,
the Good Shepherd,
the Lover of souls,

ALPHONSUS THE SINNER

consecrates this book.

Contents

To Jesus and Mary

Incarnate Word, you have given your Blood and your Life to confer on our prayers that power by which, according to your promise, they obtain for us all that we ask. And we, O God, are so careless of our salvation that we will not even ask you for the graces that we must have if we should be saved! In prayer you have given us the key of all your divine treasures; and we, rather than pray, choose to remain in our misery. Alas, O Lord, enlighten us, and make us know the value of prayers, offered in your name and by your merits, in the eyes of your Eternal Father. I consecrate to you this my book; bless it and grant that all those into whose hands it falls may have the will to pray always, and may exert themselves to stir up others also to avail themselves of this great means of salvation.

To you also do I recommend my little work, O Mary, great Mother of God; patronize it, and obtain for all who read it the spirit of prayer and of continual recourse in all their necessities to your Son, and to you who are the Dispenser of graces, the Mother of mercy, and who never leaves unsatisfied him who recommends himself to you, O mighty Virgin, but obtains from God for your servants whatever you ask.

Introduction

I have published several spiritual works on visiting the Blessed Sacrament, on the Passion of Jesus Christ, on the Glories of Mary, and besides a work against the Materialists and Deists, with other devout little treatises. Lately I brought out a work on the Infancy of our Savior entitled *Novena for Christmas*, and another entitled *Preparation for Death*, besides the one on the *Eternal Maxims*, most useful for meditation and for sermons, to which are added nine discourses suitable during seasons of divine chastisements. But I do not think that I have written a more useful work than the present, in which I speak of prayer as a necessary and certain means of obtaining salvation, and all the graces that we require for that object. If it were in my power, I would distribute a copy of it to every Catholic in the world, in order to show him the absolute necessity of prayer for salvation.

I say this because, on the one hand, I see that the absolute necessity of prayer is taught throughout the Holy Scriptures and by all the holy Fathers; while, on the other hand, I see that Christians are very careless in their practice of this great means of salvation. And, sadder still, I see that preachers take very little care to speak of it to their flocks, and confessors to their penitents; I see, moreover that even the spiritual books now popular do not speak sufficiently of it; for it is not a thing preachers and confessors and spiritual books favors. Prayer in a strict sense, says the holy Doctor, means recourse to God; but in its general signification it includes all the kinds just enumerated. It is in this latter sense that the word is used in this book.

11

PLAN OF THE WORK

In order, then, to attach ourselves to this great means of salvation, we must first of all consider how necessary it is to us, and how powerful it is to obtain for us all the graces that we can desire from God, if we know how to ask for them as we ought. Hence, in the first part, we will speak first of the necessity and power of prayer; and next, of the conditions necessary to make it efficacious with God. Then, in the second part, we will show that the grace of prayer is given to all; and there we will treat of the manner in which grace ordinarily operates.

Part I

The Necessity, Power, and Conditions of Prayer

CHAPTER I

The Necessity of Prayer

I. Prayer is a means necessary to salvation

One of the errors of Pelagianism was the assertion that prayer is not necessary for salvation. Pelagius, the impious author of that heresy, said that man will only be damned for neglecting to know the truths necessary to be learned. How astonishing! St. Augustine said, "Pelagius discussed everything except how to pray," though, as the saint held and taught, prayer is the only means of acquiring the science of the saints, according to the text of St. James: "If any man wants wisdom, let him ask of God, who gives to all abundantly and upbraids not" (James 1:5). The Scriptures are clear enough in pointing out how necessary it is to pray if we would be saved. "We ought always to pray, and not to faint" (Luke 18:1). "Watch and pray that you enter not into temptation" (Matthew 26:31). "Ask, and it shall be given you" (Matthew 7:7). The words "we ought," "pray," "ask," according to the general consent of theologians, impose the precept and denote the necessity of prayer. Wickliffe said that these texts are to be understood not precisely of prayer, but only of the necessity of good works, for in his system prayer was only well-doing; but this was his error and was expressly condemned by the Church. Hence Lessius wrote that it is heresy to deny that prayer is necessary for salvation in adults; as it evidently appears from Scripture that prayer is the means without which we cannot obtain the help necessary for salvation.[1]

The reason of this is evident. Without the assistance of God's grace we can do no good thing: "Without me, you can do nothing" (John 15:5). St. Augustine remarks on this passage that our Lord did not say, "Without me, you can complete nothing," but "without me, you can do nothing,"[2] giving us to understand that without grace we cannot even begin to do a good thing. No—more: St. Paul writes that of ourselves we cannot even have the wish to do good. "Not that we are sufficient to think anything of ourselves, but our sufficiency is from God" (2 Corinthians 3:6). If we cannot even think a good thing, much less can we wish it. The same thing is taught in many other passages of Scripture: "God works all in all" (1 Corinthians 12:6). "I will cause you to walk in my commandments, and to keep my judgments and do them" (Ezekiel 36:27). So that, as St. Leo I says, "Man does no good thing except that which God, by his grace, enables him to do,"[3] and hence the Council of Trent says, "If anyone shall assert that without the previous inspiration of the Holy Spirit and his assistance, man can believe, hope, love, or repent as he ought, in order to obtain the grace of justification, let him be anathema."[4]

The author of the *Opus Imperfectum* says that God has given to some animals swiftness, to others claws, to others wings for the preservation of their life; but he has so formed man that God himself is his only strength.[5] So that man is completely unable to provide for his own safety, since God has willed that whatever he has, or can have, should come entirely from the assistance of his grace.

But this grace is not given in God's ordinary Providence, except to those who pray for it, according to the celebrated saying of Gennadius: "We believe that no one approaches to be saved, except at the invitation of

1. *De just.*, book 2, c. 37, d. 3.
2. *Contra ep. pel.*, book 2, c. 8.
3. *Conc. Araus.*, 2, c. 20.
4. Sess. 6, c. 3.
5. Hom. 18.

God; that no one who is invited works out his salvation, except by the help of God; that no one merits this help, unless he prays."[6] From these two premises, on the one hand that we can do nothing without the assistance of grace, and on the other that this assistance is only given ordinarily by God to the man that prays, who does not see that the consequence follows that prayer is absolutely necessary to us for salvation? And although the first graces that come to us without any cooperation on our part, such as the call to faith or to penance, are, as St. Augustine says, granted by God even to those who do not pray, yet the saint considers it certain that the other graces, and specially the grace of perseverance, are not granted except in answer to prayer: "God gives us some things, such as the beginning of faith, even when we do not pray. Other things, such as perseverance, he has only provided for those who pray."[7]

Hence it is that the generality of theologians—following St. Basil, St. Chrysostom, Clement of Alexandria, St. Augustine, and other Fathers— teach that prayer is necessary to adults not only because of the obligation of the precept (as they say), but because it is necessary as a means of salvation. That is to say, in the ordinary course of Providence, it is impossible that a Christian should be saved without recommending himself to God and asking for the graces necessary to salvation. St. Thomas teaches the same: "After baptism, continual prayer is necessary to man in order that he may enter heaven; for though by baptism our sins are remitted, there still remain concupiscence to assail us from within, and the world and the devil to assail us from without."[8] The reason, then, which makes us certain of the necessity of prayer is shortly this: in order to be saved we must contend and conquer. "He who strives for the mastery is not crowned unless he strives lawfully" (2 Timothy 2:5). But without the divine assistance, we cannot resist the might of so many and so powerful enemies. Now this assistance is only granted to prayer; therefore without prayer, there is no salvation.

Moreover, that prayer is the only ordinary means of receiving the divine gifts is more distinctly proved by St. Thomas in another place, where he says that whatever graces God has from all eternity determined

6. *De Eccl. Dogm.*, c. 26.
7. *De dono pers.*, c. 16.
8. P. 3, q. 39, a. 5.

to give us, he will only give them if we pray for them. St. Gregory says the same thing: "Man by prayer merits to receive that which God had from all eternity determined to give him."[9] Not, says St. Thomas that prayer is necessary in order that God may know our necessities, but in order that we may know the necessity of having recourse to God to obtain the help necessary for our salvation, and may thus acknowledge him to be the author of all our good. As, therefore, it is God's law that we should provide ourselves with bread by sowing corn, and with wine by planting vines, so has he ordained that we should receive the graces necessary to salvation by means of prayer: "Ask, and it shall be given you; seek, and you shall find" (Matthew 7:7).

We, in a word, are merely beggars, who have nothing but what God bestows on us as alms: "But I am a beggar and poor" (Psalm 40:18). The Lord, says St. Augustine, desires and wills to pour forth his graces upon us, but will not give them except to him who prays. God wishes to give, but only gives to him who asks. This is declared in the words, "Seek, and it shall be given to you." Whence it follows, says St. Teresa, that he who seeks not, does not receive. As moisture is necessary for the life of plants to prevent them from drying up, so, says St. Chrysostom, is prayer necessary for our salvation. Or, as he says in another place, prayer vivifies the soul as the soul vivifies the body: "As the body without the soul cannot live, so the soul without prayer is dead and emits an offensive odor."[10] He uses these words because the man who omits to recommend himself to God at once begins to be defiled with sins. Prayer is also called the food of the soul, because the body cannot be supported without food; nor can the soul, says St. Augustine, be kept alive without prayer: "As the flesh is nourished by food, so is man supported by prayers."[11] All these comparisons used by the holy Fathers are intended by them to teach the absolute necessity of prayer for the salvation of everyone.

---

9. *Dial.*, book 1, c. 8.
10. *De or. D.*, book 1.
11. *De sal. Doc.*, c. 28.

II.   Without prayer it is impossible to resist temptations and to keep the commandments

Moreover, prayer is the most necessary weapon of defense against our enemies; he who does not avail himself of it, says St. Thomas, is lost. He does not doubt that the reason of Adam's fall was because he did not recommend himself to God when he was tempted: "He sinned because he had not recourse to the divine assistance."[12] St. Gelasius says the same of the rebel angels: "Receiving the grace of God in vain, they could not persevere because they did not pray."[13] St. Charles Borromeo, in a pastoral letter, observes that among all the means of salvation recommended by Jesus Christ in the Gospel, the first place is given to prayer; and he has determined that this should distinguish his Church from all false religions when he calls her "the house of prayer": "My house is a house of prayer" (Matthew 21:13). St. Charles concludes that prayer is "the beginning and progress and the completion of all virtues."[14] So that in darkness, distress, and danger, we have no other hope than to raise our eyes to God, and with fervent prayers to beseech his mercy to save us: "As we know not," said king Jehoshaphat, "what to do, we can only turn our eyes to you" (2 Chronicles 20:12). This also was David's practice, who could find no other means of safety from his enemies than continual prayer to God to deliver him from their snares: "My eyes are ever toward the Lord; for he shall pluck my feet out of the snare" (Psalm 25:15). So he did nothing but pray: "Look upon me, and have mercy on me; for I am alone and poor." (Psalm 25:16). "I cried unto you, O Lord; save me, that I may keep your commandments" (Psalm 119:146). Lord, turn your eyes to me, have pity on me, and save me; for I can do nothing, and beside you there is none that can help me.

And, indeed how could we ever resist our enemies and observe God's precepts, especially since Adam's sin, which has rendered us so weak and infirm, unless we had prayer as a means whereby we can obtain from God sufficient light and strength to enable us to observe them? It was a blasphemy of Luther's to say that after the sin of Adam the observance

---

12.   P. 1, q. 94, a. 4.
13.   *Tr. Adv. Pelag. Haer.*
14.   *Litt. Past. de or. in comm.*

of God's law has become absolutely impossible to man. Jansen also said that there are some precepts which are impossible even to the just, with the power which they actually have, and so far his proposition bears a good sense; but it was justly condemned by the Church for the addition he made to it when he said that they have not the grace to make the precepts possible. It is true, says St. Augustine, that man, in consequence of his weakness, is unable to fulfill some of God's commands with his present strength and the ordinary grace given to all men; but he can easily, by prayer, obtain such further aid as he requires for his salvation: "God commands not impossibilities, but by commanding he suggests to you to do what you can, to ask for what is beyond your strength; and he helps you that you may be able." This is a celebrated text, which was afterward adopted and made a doctrine of faith by the Council of Trent.[15] The holy Doctor immediately adds, "Let us see whence" (i.e., how man is enabled to do that which he cannot). "By medicine he can do that which his natural weakness renders impossible to him."[16] That is, by prayer we may obtain a remedy for our weakness; for when we pray, God gives us strength to do that which we cannot do of ourselves. We cannot believe, continues St. Augustine, that God would have imposed on us the observance of a law and then made the law impossible. When, therefore, God shows us that of ourselves we are unable to observe all his commands, it is simply to admonish us to do the easier things by means of the ordinary grace which he bestows on us, and then to do the more difficult things by means of the greater help which we can obtain by prayer. "By the very fact that it is absurd to suppose that God could have commanded us to do impossible things, we are admonished what to do in easy matters and what to ask for in difficulties."[17] But why, it will be asked, has God commanded us to do things impossible to our natural strength? Precisely for this, says St. Augustine: that we may be incited to pray for help to do that which of ourselves we cannot do. "He commands some things which we cannot do, so that we may know what we ought to ask of him."[18] And in another place: "The law was given that grace might be sought for; grace was given

---

15. Sess. 6, c. 11.
16. *De Natura et gr.*, c. 43.
17. *De Natura et gr.*, c. 69.
18. *De Gr. et Lib. Arb.*, c. 16

that the law might be fulfilled."[19] The law cannot be kept without grace, and God has given the law with this object that we may always ask him for grace to observe it. In another place he says: "The law is good, if it be used lawfully; what then, is the lawful use of the law?" He answers, "When by the law we perceive our own weakness and ask of God the grace to heal us."[20] St. Augustine then says: "We ought to use the law; but for what purpose? To learn by means of the law, which we find to be above our strength, our own inability to observe it, in order that we may then obtain by prayer the divine aid to cure our weakness."

St. Bernard's teaching is the same: "What are we, or what is our strength that we should be able to resist so many temptations? This certainly it was that God intended: that we, seeing our deficiencies and that we have no other help, should with all humility have recourse to his mercy."[21] God knows how useful it is to us to be obliged to pray, in order to keep us humble and to exercise our confidence, and he therefore permits us to be assaulted by enemies too mighty to be overcome by our own strength, so that by prayer we may obtain from his mercy aid to resist them; and it is especially to be remarked that no one can resist the impure temptations of the flesh without recommending himself to God when he is tempted. This foe is so terrible that, when he fights with us, he, as it were, takes away all light; he makes us forget all our meditations, all our good resolutions; he makes us also disregard the truths of faith and even almost lose the fear of the divine punishments. For he conspires with our natural inclinations, which drive us with the greatest violence to the indulgence of sensual pleasures. He who in such a moment does not have recourse to God is lost. The only defense against this temptation is prayer, as St. Gregory of Nyssa says: "Prayer is the bulwark of chastity";[22] and before him Solomon: "And as I knew that I could not otherwise be continent except God gave it, I went to the Lord and besought him" (Wisdom 8:21). Chastity is a virtue which we have not strength to practice unless God gives it us; and God does not give this strength except to him who asks for it. But whoever prays for it will certainly obtain it.

19. *De Spir. et Litt.*, c. 19.
20. Serm. 156, Ed. Ben.
21. *In Quad.*, s. 5.
22. *De Or. Dom.*, 1.

Hence St. Thomas observes (in contradiction to Jansen) that we ought not to say that the precept of chastity, or any other, is impossible to us; for though we cannot observe it by our own strength, we can by God's assistance. "We must say that what we can do with the divine assistance is not altogether impossible to us."[23] Nor let it be said that it appears an injustice to order a cripple to walk straight. No, says St. Augustine, it is not an injustice, provided always means are given him to find the remedy for his lameness; for after this, if he continues to go crooked, the fault is his own. "It is most wisely commanded that man should walk uprightly, so that when he sees that he cannot do so of himself, he may seek a remedy to heal the lameness of sin."[24] Finally, the same holy Doctor says that he will never know how to live well who does not know how to pray well. "He knows how to live aright who knows how to pray aright."[25] And, on the other hand, St. Francis of Assisi says that without prayer you can never hope to find good fruit in a soul.

Wrongly, therefore, do those sinners excuse themselves who say that they have no strength to resist temptation. But if you have not this strength, why do you not ask for it, is the reproof which St. James gives them: "You have it not, because you ask it not" (James 4:2). There is no doubt that we are too weak to resist the attacks of our enemies. But, on the other hand, it is certain that God is faithful, as the Apostle says, and will not permit us to be tempted beyond our strength: "God is faithful, who will not suffer you to be tempted above that which you are able; but will make also with the temptation issue that you may be able to bear it" (1 Corinthians 10:13). "He will provide an issue for it," says Primasius, "by the protection of his grace that you may be able to with stand the temptation." We are weak, but God is strong; when we ask him for aid, he communicates his strength to us; and we shall be able to do all things, as the Apostle reasonably assured himself: "I can do all things in him who strengthens me" (Philippians 4:13). He, therefore, who falls has no excuse (says St. Chrysostom), because he has neglected to pray; for if he had prayed, he would not have been overcome by his enemies. "Nor

23. *Summa*, 1.2, q. 109, a. 4.
24. *De Perf. Just. hom.*, c. 3.
25. Serm. 55, E. B. app.

can any one be excused who, by ceasing to pray, has shown that he did not wish to overcome his enemy."[26]

III.   Invocation of the saints

1. IS IT GOOD AND USEFUL TO HAVE RECOURSE TO THE INTERCESSION OF THE SAINTS?

Here a question arises whether it is necessary to have recourse also to the intercession of the saints to obtain the grace of God.

That it is a lawful and useful thing to invoke the saints, as intercessors, to obtain for us, by the merits of Jesus Christ, that which we by our demerits are not worthy to receive, is a doctrine of the Church declared by the Council of Trent. "It is good and useful to invoke them by supplication, and to fly to their aid and assistance to obtain benefits from God through his Son Jesus Christ."[27]

Such invocation was condemned by the impious Calvin, but most illogically. For if it is lawful and profitable to invoke living saints to aid us and to beseech them to assist us in prayers—as the Prophet Baruch did, "And pray you for us to the Lord our God" (Baruch 1:13), and St. Paul, "Brethren, pray for us" (1 Thessalonians 5:25), and as God himself commanded the friends of Job to recommend themselves to his prayers that by the merits of Job he might look favorably on them, "Go to my servant Job . . . and my servant Job shall pray for you; his face I will accept" (Job 42:8)—if, then, it is lawful to recommend ourselves to the living, how can it be unlawful to invoke the saints who in heaven enjoy God face to face? This is not derogatory to the honor due to God, but it is doubling it; for it is honoring the king not only in his person but in his servants. Therefore, says St. Thomas, it is good to have recourse to many saints, "Because by the prayers of many we can sometimes obtain that which we cannot by the prayers of one." And if anyone objects, "But why have recourse to the saints to pray for us, when they are already praying for all who are worthy of it?" the same Doctor answers that no one can be said

---

26.   *Serm. de Moyse.*
27.   Sess. 25, *De inv. Sanct.*

to be worthy that the saints should pray for him; but that "he becomes worthy by having recourse to the saint with devotion."[28]

2. IS IT GOOD TO INVOKE ALSO THE SOULS IN PURGATORY?

Again, it is disputed whether there is any use in recommending one's self to the souls in purgatory. Some say that the souls in that state cannot pray for us; and these rely on the authority of St. Thomas, who says that those souls, while they are being purified by pain, are inferior to us and therefore "are not in a state to pray for us, but rather require our prayers."[29] But many other Doctors, such as Bellarmine,[30] Sylvius,[31] Cardinal Gotti,[32] Lessius,[33] Medina, and others affirm with great probability that we should piously believe that God manifests our prayer to those holy souls in order that they may pray for us; and that so the charitable interchange of mutual prayer may be kept up between them and us. Nor do St. Thomas's words present much difficulty; for, as Sylvius and Gotti say, it is one thing not to be in a state to pray, another not to be able to pray. It is true that those souls are not in a state to pray because, as St. Thomas says, while suffering they are inferior to us and rather require our prayers; nevertheless, in this state they are well able to pray, as they are friends of God. If a father keeps a son whom he tenderly loves in confinement for some fault—if the son then is not in a state to pray for himself—is that any reason why he cannot pray for others? And may he not expect to obtain what he asks, knowing, as he does, his father's affection for him? So the souls in purgatory, being beloved by God and confirmed in grace, have absolutely no impediment to prevent them from praying for us. Still the Church does not invoke them or implore their intercession, because ordinarily they have no cognizance of our prayers. But we may piously believe that God makes our prayers known to them; and then they, full of charity as they are, most assuredly do not omit to pray for us. St. Catherine of Bologna, whenever she desired any favor, had recourse to the souls in purgatory,

---

28. *In 4 Sent.,* dist. 45, q. 3, a. 2.
29. *Summa,* 1.2, q. 83, a. 11.
30. *De Purg.,* book 2, c. 15.
31. *In Suppl.,* q. 71, q. 6.
32. *De St. an. p. vit.,* q. 4, d. 2.
33. *De Just.,* book 2, c. 37, d. 5.

and was immediately heard. She even testified that by the intercession of the souls in purgatory she had obtained many graces which she had not been able to obtain by the intercession of the saints.

3. IT IS OUR DUTY TO PRAY FOR THE SOULS IN PURGATORY

But here let me make a digression in favor of those holy souls. If we desire the aid of their prayers, it is but fair that we should mind to aid them with our prayers and good works. I said it is fair, but I should have said it is a Christian duty; for charity obliges us to succor our neighbor when he requires our aid, and we can help him without grievous inconvenience. Now it is certain that among our neighbors are to be reckoned the souls in purgatory, who, although no longer living in this world, yet have not left the communion of saints. "The souls of the pious dead," says St. Augustine, "are not separated from the Church,"[34] and St. Thomas says more to our purpose that the charity which is due to the dead who died in the grace of God is only an extension of the same charity which we owe to our neighbor while living: "Charity, which is the bond which unites the members of the Church, extends not only to the living, but also to the dead who die in charity."[35] Therefore, we ought to succor, according to our ability, those holy souls as our neighbors; and as their necessities are greater than those of our other neighbors, for this reason our duty to succor them seems also to be greater.

But now, what are the necessities of those holy prisoners? It is certain that their pains are immense. The fire that tortures them, says St. Augustine, is more excruciating than any pain that man can endure in this life: "That fire will be more painful than anything that man can suffer in this life."[36] St. Thomas thinks the same, and supposes it to be identical with the fire of hell: "The damned are tormented and the elect purified in the same fire."[37] And this only relates to the pains of sense. But the pain of loss (that is, the privation of the sight of God) which those holy souls suffer is much greater, because not only their natural affection, but also the supernatural love of God, wherewith they burn, draws them with

---

34. *De Civitate Dei*, book 2, c. 9.
35. *In 4 Sent.*, d. 45, q. 2, s. 2.
36. *In Ps.* 37.
37. *In 4 Sent.*, d. 21, q. 1, a. 1.

such violence to be united with their Sovereign Good that when they see the barrier which their sins have put in the way, they feel a pain so acute that if they were capable of death, they could not live a moment. So that, as St. Chrysostom says, this pain of the deprivation of God tortures them incomparably more than the pain of sense: "The flames of a thousand hells together could not inflict such torments as the pain of loss by itself." So that those holy souls would rather suffer every other possible torture than be deprived for a single instant of the union with God for which they long. So St. Thomas says that the pain of purgatory exceeds anything that can be endured in this life: "The pain of purgatory must exceed all pain of this life."[38] And Dionysius the Carthusian relates that a dead person who had been raised to life by the intercession of St. Jerome told St. Cyril of Jerusalem that all the torments of this earth are refreshing and delightful when compared with the very least pain of purgatory: "If all the torments of the world were compared with the least that can be had in purgatory, they would appear comfortable."[39] And he adds that if a man had once tried those torments, he would rather suffer all the earthly sorrows that man can endure till the Day of Judgment than suffer for one day the least pain of purgatory. Hence St. Cyril wrote to St. Augustine: "As far as regards the infliction of suffering, these pains are the same as those of hell, their only difference being that they are not eternal."[40] Hence we see that the pains of these holy souls are excessive, while, on the other hand, they cannot help themselves; because as Job says, "They are in chains, and are bound with the cords of poverty" (Job 36:8). They are destined to reign with Christ; but they are withheld from taking possession of their kingdom till the time of their purgation is accomplished. And they cannot help themselves (at least not sufficiently, even according to those theologians who assert that they can by their prayers gain some relief) to throw off their chains until they have entirely satisfied the justice of God. This is precisely what a Cistercian monk said to the sacristan of his monastery: "Help me, I beseech you, with your prayers; for of myself I can obtain nothing." And this is consistent with the saying of St. Bonaventure: "Destitution prevents

38. *Loc. cit.*
39. *De Quat. Nov.*, a. 53.
40. *Int. Op. Aug. Ep.* 19, E. B. app.

solvency."[41] That is, those souls are so poor that they have no means of making satisfaction. On the other hand, since it is certain and even of faith that by our suffrages, and chiefly by our prayers, as particularly recommended and practiced by the Church, we can relieve those holy souls, I do not know how to excuse that man from sin who neglects to give them some assistance, at least by his prayers. If a sense of duty will not persuade us to succor them, let us think of the pleasure it will give Jesus Christ to see us endeavoring to deliver his beloved spouses from prison, in order that he may have them with him in paradise. Let us think of the store of merit which we can lay up by practicing this great act of charity; let us think, too that those souls are not ungrateful and will never forget the great benefit we do them in relieving them of their pains and in obtaining for them, by our prayers, anticipation of their entrance into glory; so that when they are there they will never neglect to pray for us. And if God promises mercy to him who practices mercy toward his neighbor—"Blessed are the merciful, for they shall obtain mercy" (Matthew 5:7)—he may reasonably expect to be saved who remembers to assist those souls so afflicted and yet so dear to God. Jonathan, after having saved the Hebrews from ruin by a victory over their enemies, was condemned to death by his father, Saul, for having tasted some honey against his express commands; but the people came before the king and said, "Shall Jonathan then die, who has wrought this great salvation in Israel?" (1 Samuel 14:45). So may we expect that if any of us ever obtains, by his prayers, the liberation of a soul from purgatory, that soul will say to God, "Lord, do not allow him who has delivered me from my torments to be lost." And if Saul spared Jonathan's life at the request of his people, God will not refuse the salvation of a Christian to the prayers of a soul which is his own spouse. Moreover, St. Augustine says that God will cause those who in this life have most succored those holy souls, when they come to purgatory themselves, to be most succored by others. I may here observe that, in practice, one of the best suffrages is to hear Mass for them and during the Holy Sacrifice to recommend them to God by the merits and Passion of Jesus Christ. The following form may be used: "Eternal Father, I offer you this Sacrifice of the Body and Blood of Jesus

---

41. *Serm. de mort.*

Christ, with all the pains which he suffered in his life and death; and by his Passion I recommend to you the souls in Purgatory, and especially that of . . . " etc. And it is a very charitable act to recommend, at the same time, the souls of all those who are at the point of death.

4. IS IT NECESSARY TO INVOKE THE SAINTS?

Whatever doubt there may be whether or not the souls in purgatory can pray for us, and therefore whether or not it is of any use to recommend ourselves to their prayers, there can be no doubt whatever with regard to the saints. For it is certain that it is most useful to have recourse to the intercession of the saints canonized by the Church, who are already enjoying the vision of God. To suppose that the Church can err in canonizing is a sin or is heresy, according to St. Bonaventure, Bellarmine, and others; or at least next door to heresy, according to Suarez, Azorius, Gotti, etc., because the Sovereign Pontiff, according to St. Thomas, is guided by the infallible influence of the Holy Spirit in an especial way when canonizing the saints.[42]

But to return to the question just proposed: Are we obliged to have recourse to the intercession of the saints? I do not wish to meddle with the decision of this question, but I cannot omit the exposition of a doctrine of St. Thomas. In several places above quoted, and especially in his book of *Sentences*, he expressly lays it down as certain that everyone is bound to pray because (as he asserts) in no other way can the graces necessary for salvation be obtained from God, except by prayer: "Every man is bound to pray, from the fact that he is bound to procure spiritual good for himself, which can only be got from God; so it can only be obtained by asking it of God."[43] Then, in another place of the same book, he proposes the exact question, "Whether we are bound to pray to the saints to intercede for us?"[44] And he answers as follows in order to catch his real meaning—we will quote the entire passage—"According to Dionysius, the order which God has instituted for his creatures requires that things which are remote may be brought to God by means of things which are nearer to him. Hence, as the saints in heaven are nearest of all to him, the

---

42. *Quodl.* 9, a. 16, ad 1.
43. *In 4 Sent.*, d. 15, q. 4, a. 1.
44. Dist. 45, q. 3, a. 2.

order of his law requires that we, who remaining in the body are absent from the Lord, should be brought to him by means of the saints; and this is effected by the divine goodness pouring forth his gifts through them. And as the path of our return to God should correspond to the path of the good things which proceed from him to us, it follows that, as the benefits of God come down to us by means of the suffrages of the saints, we ought to be brought to God by the same way, so that a second time we may receive his benefits by the mediation of the saints. Hence it is that we make them our intercessors with God and, as it were, our mediators, when we ask them to pray for us." Note well the words "the order of God's law requires," and especially note the last words "as the benefits of God come down to us by means of the suffrages of the saints, in the same way we must be brought back to God so that a second time we may receive his benefits by the mediation of the saints." So that, according to St. Thomas, the order of the divine law requires that we mortals should be saved by means of the saints, in that we receive by their intercession the help necessary for our salvation. He then puts the objection that it appears superfluous to have recourse to the saints, since God is infinitely more merciful than they and more ready to hear us. This he answers by saying: "God has so ordered, not on account of any want of mercy on his part, but to keep the right order which he has universally established, of working by means of second causes. It is not for want of his mercy, but to preserve the aforesaid order in the creation."

In conformity with this doctrine of St. Thomas, the Continuator of Tourneley and Sylvius writes that although God only is to be prayed to as the Author of grace, yet we are bound to have recourse also to the intercession of the saints, so as to observe the order which God has established with regard to our salvation, which is that the inferior should be saved by imploring the aid of the superior. "By the law of nature we are bound to observe the order which God has appointed; but God has appointed that the inferior should obtain salvation by imploring the assistance of his superior."[45]

---

45.   *De Relig.*, p. 2, c. 2, a. 5.

IV. The intercession of the Blessed Virgin

And if this is true of the saints, much more is it true of the intercession
of the Mother of God, whose prayers are certainly of more value in his
sight than those of all the rest of the inhabitants of heaven together. For
St. Thomas says that the saints, in proportion to the merits by which they
have obtained grace for themselves, are able also to save others, but that
Jesus Christ, and so also his Mother, have merited so much grace that they
can save all men. "It is a great thing in any saint that he should have grace
enough for the salvation of many beside himself; but if he had enough for
the salvation of all men, this would be the greatest of all; and this is the
case with Christ, and with the Blessed Virgin."[46] And St. Bernard speaks
thus to Mary: "Through you we have access to your Son, O discoverer
of grace and Mother of salvation, that through you he may receive us,
who through you was given to us."[47] These words signify that as we only
have access to the Father by means of the Son, who is the Mediator of
justice, so we only have access to the Son by means of the Mother, who is
mediator of grace, and who obtains for us, by her intercession, the gifts
which Jesus Christ has merited for us. And therefore St. Bernard says, in
another place, that Mary has received a twofold fullness of grace. The first
was the Incarnation of the Word, who was made Man in her most holy
womb; the second is that fullness of grace which we receive from God by
means of her prayers. Hence the saint adds, "God has placed the fullness
of all good in Mary, so that if we have any hope, any grace, any salvation,
we may know that it overflows from her who ascends abounding with
delights."[48] She is a garden of delights, whose odors spread abroad and
abound—that is, the gifts of graces. So that whatever good we have from
God, we receive all by the intercession of Mary. And why so? Because, says
St. Bernard, it is God's will: "Such is his will, who would have us receive
everything through Mary." But the more precise reason is deduced from
the expression of St. Augustine that Mary is justly called our Mother
because she cooperated by her charity in the birth of the faithful to the
life of grace, by which we become members of Jesus Christ, our head:

46. *Expos. in Sal. Ang.*
47. *In Adv. Dom.*, s. 2.
48. *De Aquaed.*

"But clearly she is the mother of his members (which we are); because she cooperated by her charity in the birth of the faithful in the Church, and they are members of that Head."[49] Therefore, as Mary cooperated by her charity in the spiritual birth of the faithful, so also God willed that she should cooperate by her intercession to make them enjoy the life of grace in this world, and the life of glory in the next; and therefore the Church makes us call her and salute her, without any circumlocution, by the names, "our life, our sweetness, and our hope."

Hence St. Bernard exhorts us to have continual recourse to the Mother of God because her prayers are certain to be heard by her Son: "Go to Mary, I say, without hesitation; the Son will hear the Mother." And then he says, "My children, she is the ladder of sinners, she is my chief confidence, she is the whole ground of my hope."[50] He calls her "ladder" because, as you cannot mount the third step except you first put your foot on the second, nor can you arrive at the second except by the first, so you cannot come to God except by means of Jesus Christ, nor can you come to Christ except by means of his Mother. Then he calls her "his greatest security, and the whole ground of his hope" because, as he affirms, God wills that all the graces which he gives us should pass through the hands of Mary. And he concludes by saying that we ought to ask all the graces which we desire through Mary because she obtains whatever she seeks, and her prayers cannot be rejected. "Let us seek grace, and let us seek it through Mary, because what she seeks she finds, and she cannot be disappointed." The following saints teach the same as St. Bernard: St. Ephrem, "We have no other confidence than from you, O purest Virgin!"[51] St. Ildephonsus, "All the good things that the divine Majesty has determined to give them, he has determined to commit to your hands; for to you are entrusted the treasures and the wardrobes of grace."[52] St. Germanus, "If you desert us, what will become of us, O life of Christians?"[53] St. Peter Damian, "In your hands are all the treasures

---

49. *De S. Virginit.*, c. 6.
50. *De Aquaed.*
51. *De Laud. B. M. V.*
52. *De Cor. Virg.*, c. 15.
53. *De zona Deip.*

of the mercies of God."[54] St. Antoninus, "Who seeks without her aid, attempts to fly without wings."[55] St. Bernardine of Sienna, "You are the dispenser of all graces; our salvation is in your hands." In another place he not only says that all graces are transmitted to us by means of Mary, but he also asserts that the Blessed Virgin, from the time she became Mother of God, acquired a certain jurisdiction over all the graces that are given to us. "Through the Virgin the vital graces are transfused from Christ, the Head, into his mystical body." From the time when the Virgin Mother conceived in her womb the Word of God, she obtained a certain jurisdiction (if I may so speak) over every temporal procession of the Holy Spirit; so that no creature could obtain any grace from God except by the dispensation of his sweet Mother." And he concludes, "Therefore all gifts, virtues, and graces are dispensed through her hands to whom she wills, and as she wills."[56] St. Bonaventure says the same: "Since the whole divine nature was in the womb of the Virgin, I do not fear to teach that she has a certain jurisdiction over all the streams of grace; as her womb was, as it were, an ocean of the divine nature, whence all the streams of grace must emanate." On the authority of these saints, many theologians have piously and reasonably defended the opinion that there is no grace given to us except by means of the intercession of Mary; so Mendoza, Vega, Paciucchelli, Segneri, Poire, Crasset, and others, as also the learned Alexander Natalis, who says: "It is God's will that we should look to him for all good things, to be procured by the most powerful intercession of the Blessed Virgin when we invoke her, as it is fit."[57] And he quotes in confirmation the passage of St. Bernard: "Such is his will, who has determined that we should receive all through Mary."[58] Contenson says the same in a comment on the words addressed by Jesus on the cross to St. John, "Behold your Mother" (John 19:27). As though he had said, "No one shall be partaker of my blood except by the intercession of my Mother. My wounds are fountains of grace; but their streams shall flow to no one except through the canal of Mary. O my disciple John, I will love

---

54. *De Nativ.*, s. 1.
55. P. 4, tit. 15, c. 22.
56. *S. d. Nat. M. V.*, c. 8.
57. *Ep.* 50, *in calce Theol.*
58. *De Aquaed.*

you as you love her!"[59] For the rest, it is certain that if God is pleased when we have recourse to the saints, he will be much more pleased when we avail ourselves of the intercession of Mary, so that she, by her merits, may compensate for our unworthiness, according to the words of St. Anselm: "That the dignity of the intercessor may supply for our poverty. So that to invoke the Virgin is not to distrust God's mercy, but to fear our own unworthiness."[60] St. Thomas, speaking of her dignity, calls it, as it were, infinite: "From the fact that she is the Mother of God, she has a certain infinite dignity."[61] So that it may be said with reason that the prayers of Mary have more power with God than those of all heaven together.

Conclusion of the chapter

Let us conclude this first point by giving the gist of all that has been said hitherto. He who prays is certainly saved. He who does not pray is certainly damned. All the blessed (except infants) have been saved by prayer. All the damned have been lost through not praying; if they had prayed, they would not have been lost. And this is, and will be, their greatest torment in hell: to think how easily they might have been saved, only by asking God for his grace; but that now it is too late, the time of prayer is over.

---

59. *Theol. ment. et cord.*, vol. 2, book 10, d. 4, c.
60. *De incarn.*, q. 37, a. 4, d. 23, s. 3.
61. P. 1, q. 25, a. 6, ad 4.

CHAPTER II

The Power of Prayer

I.   Excellence of prayer and its power with God

Our prayers are so dear to God that he has appointed the angels to present them to him as soon as they come forth from our mouths. "The angels," says St. Hilary, "preside over the prayers of the faithful and offer them daily to God."[62] This is that smoke of the incense, which are the prayers of saints, which St. John saw ascending to God from the hands of the angels (Revelation 8:3), and which he saw in another place represented by golden phials full of sweet odors, very acceptable to God. But in order to understand better the value of prayers in God's sight, it is sufficient to read both in the Old and New Testaments the innumerable promises which God makes to the man who prays. "Cry to me, and I will hear you" (Psalm 50:15). "Call upon me, and I will deliver you" (Jeremiah 33:3). "Ask, and it shall be given you; seek, and you shall find; knock, and it shall be opened unto you. He shall give good things to them that ask him" (Matthew 7:7). "Everyone that asks receives, and he that seeks finds" (Luke 11:10). "Whatsoever they shall ask, it shall be done for them by my Father" (John 15:7). "All things whatsoever you ask when you pray, believe that you shall receive them, and they shall come unto you" (Matthew 18:19). "If you ask me anything in my name, that will I do" (Mark 11:24). "You shall ask whatever you will, and it shall be done unto you. Amen, amen, I say unto you, if you ask the Father anything in my name, he will give it you" (John 14:14 and 16:23). There are a thousand similar texts; but it would take too long to quote them.

    God wills us to be saved; but for our greater good, he wills us to be

62.   *In Matt. Can.* 18.

saved as conquerors. While, therefore, we remain here, we have to live in a continual warfare; and if we should be saved, we have to fight and conquer. "No one can be crowned without victory," says St. Chrysostom.[63] We are very feeble, and our enemies are many and mighty; how shall we be able to stand against them, or to defeat them? Let us take courage, and say with the Apostle, "I can do all things in him who strengthens me" (Philippians 4:13). By prayer we can do all things; for by this means God will give us that strength which we want. Theodoret says that prayer is omnipotent; it is but one, yet it can do all things: "Though prayer is one, it can do all things."[64] And St. Bonaventure asserts that by prayer we obtain every good and escape every evil: "By it is obtained the gain of every good and liberation from every evil."[65] St. Laurence Justinian says that by means of prayer we build for ourselves a strong tower, where we shall be secure from all the snares and assaults of our enemies: "By the exercise of prayer man is able to erect a citadel for himself."[66] The powers of hell are mighty," says St. Bernard, "but prayer is stronger than all the devils."[67] Yes; for by prayer the soul obtains God's help, which is stronger than any created power. Thus David encouraged himself in his alarms: "Praising I will call upon the Lord, and I shall be saved from my enemies" (Psalm 18:4). For, as St. Chrysostom says, "Prayer is a strong weapon, a defense, a port, and a treasure."[68] It is a weapon sufficient to overcome every assault of the devil; it is a defense to preserve us in every danger; it is a port where we may be safe in every tempest; and it is at the same time a treasure which provides us with every good.

II. Power of prayer against temptation

God knows the great good which it does us to be obliged to pray and therefore permits us (as we have already shown in the previous chapter) to be assaulted by our enemies, in order that we may ask him for the help

---

63. *De Mart.*, s. 1.
64. *Ap. Rodrig.*, p. 1, tr. 5, c. 14.
65. *In Luc.*, 11.
66. *De Cast. Conn.*, c. 22.
67. *De Modo bene viv.*, s. 49.
68. *Hom. in Ps.* 145.

which he offers and promises to us. But as he is pleased when we run to him in our dangers, so is he displeased when he sees us neglectful of prayer. "As the king," says St. Bonaventure, "would think it faithlessness in an officer, when his post was attacked, not to ask him for reinforcements, he would be reputed a traitor if he did not request help from the king,"[69] so God thinks himself betrayed by the man who, when he finds himself surrounded by temptations, does not run to him for assistance. For he desires to help us and only waits to be asked, and then gives abundant succor. This is strikingly shown by Isaiah, when, on God's part, he told the king Ahaz to ask some sign to assure himself of God's readiness to help him: "Ask a sign of the Lord your God" (Isaiah 7:11). The faithless king answered, "I will not ask, and I will not tempt the Lord," for he trusted in his own power to overcome his enemies without God's aid. And for this the Prophet reproved him, "Hear, therefore, O house of David: is it a small thing for you to be grievous to men that you are grievous to my God also?" because that man is grievous and offensive to God who will not ask him for the graces which he offers.

"Come to me, all you that labor and are burdened, and I will refresh you" (Matthew 11:28). "My poor children," says our Savior, "though you find yourselves assailed by enemies and oppressed with the weight of your sins, do not lose heart, but have recourse to me in prayer, and I will give you strength to resist, and I will give you a remedy for all your disasters." In another place he says, by the mouth of Isaiah, "Come and accuse me, says the Lord; if your sins are as scarlet, they shall be made white as snow" (Isaiah 1:18). O men, come to me; though your consciences are horribly defiled, yet come; I even give you leave to reproach me (so to speak) if, after you have had recourse to me, I do not give you grace to become white as snow.

What is prayer? It is, as St. Chrysostom says, "the anchor of those tossed on the sea, the treasure of the poor, the cure of diseases, the safeguard of health."[70] It is a secure anchor for him who is in peril of shipwreck; it is a treasury of immense wealth for him who is poor; it is a most efficacious medicine for him who is sick; and it is a certain

69. *Diaeta sal.*, vol. 2, c. 5.
70. *Hom. de Consubst. cont. Anom.*

preservative for him who would keep himself well. What does prayer effect? Let us hear St. Laurence Justinian: "It pleases God, it gets what it asks, it overcomes enemies, it changes men."[71] It appeases the wrath of God, who pardons all who pray with humility. It obtains every grace that is asked for; it vanquishes all the strength of the tempter; and it changes men from blind into seeing, from weak into strong, from sinners into saints. Let him who wants light ask it of God, and it shall be given. As soon as I had recourse to God, says Solomon, he granted me wisdom: "I called upon God, and the Spirit of wisdom came to me" (Wisdom 7:7). Let him who wants fortitude ask it of God, and it shall be given. As soon as I opened my mouth to pray, says David, I received help from God: "I opened my month, and drew in the Spirit" (Psalm 119:131). And how in the world did the martyrs obtain strength to resist tyrants, except by prayer, which gave them force to overcome dangers and death?

"He who uses this great weapon," says St. Chrysostom, "knows not death, leaves the earth, enters heaven, lives with God."[72] He does not fall into sin; he loses affection for the earth; he makes his abode in heaven and begins, even in this life, to enjoy the conversation of God. How, then, can you disquiet such a man by saying, "How do you know that you are written in the book of life?" How do you know whether God will give you efficacious grace and the gift of perseverance? "Be nothing solicitous," says St. Paul, "but in everything by prayer and supplication, with thanksgiving, let your petitions be known unto God" (Philippians 4:6). What is the use, says the Apostle, of agitating yourselves with these miseries and fears? Drive from you all these cares, which are of no use but to lessen your confidence and to make you more tepid and slothful in walking along the way of salvation. Pray and seek always, and make your prayers sound in God's ears, and thank him for having promised to give you the gifts which you desire whenever you ask for them, namely, efficacious grace, perseverance, salvation, and everything that you desire. The Lord has given us our post in the battle against powerful foes; but he is faithful in his promises and will never allow us to be assaulted more violently than we can resist: "God is faithful, who will not allow

---

71. *De Perf.*, c. 12.
72. Serm. 45.

you to be tempted above that which you are able" (1 Corinthians 10:13). He is faithful, since he instantly succors the man who invokes him. The learned Cardinal Gotti writes that God has bound himself not only to give us grace precisely balancing the temptation that assails us, but that he is obliged, when we are tempted and have recourse to him, to afford us, by means of that grace which is kept ready for and offered to all, sufficient strength for us actually to resist the temptation. "God is bound, when we are tempted and fly to his protection, to give us, by the grace prepared and offered to all, such strength as will not only put us in the way of being able to resist, but will also make us resist; for 'we can do all things in him who strengthens us by his grace,' if we humbly ask for it."[73] We can do all things with God's help, which is granted to everyone who humbly seeks it; so that we have no excuse when we allow ourselves to be overcome by a temptation. We are conquered solely by our own fault, because we would not pray. By prayer all the snares and power of the devil are easily overcome. "By prayer all hurtful things are chased away," says St. Augustine.[74]

III.   God is always ready to hear us

St. Bernardine of Sienna says that prayer is a faithful ambassador, well known to the King of Heaven, and having access to his private chamber and able by his importunity to induce the merciful heart of the King to grant every aid to us, his wretched creatures, groaning in the midst of our conflicts and miseries in this valley of tears. "Prayer is a most faithful messenger, known to the King, who is used to enter his chamber and by his importunity to influence the merciful mind of the King, and to obtain us assistance in our toils."[75] Isaiah also assures us that as soon as the Lord hears our prayers, he is moved with compassion toward us, and does not leave us to cry long to him, but instantly replies and grants us what we ask: "Weeping, you shall not weep; he will surely have pity upon you: the voice of your cry as soon as he shall hear, he will answer you" (Isaiah 30:19). In another place he complains of us by the mouth of

73.   *De Grat.*, q. 2, d. 5, s. 3.
74.   *De Sal. Doc.*, c. 28.
75.   *T. 4. s. in Dom. 5. p. Pasc.*

Jeremiah: "Am I become a wilderness to Israel, or a lateward springing land? Why then have my people said, 'We are revolted and will come to you no more'?" (Jeremiah 2:31). Why do you say that you will no more have recourse to me? Has my mercy become to you a barren land, which can yield you no fruits of grace? Or a cold soil, which yields its fruit too late? So has our loving Lord assured us that he never neglects to hear us, and to hear us instantly when we pray; and so does he reproach those who neglect to pray through distrust of being heard.

If God were to allow us to present our petitions to him once a month, even this would be a great favor. The kings of the earth give audiences a few times in the year, but God gives a continual audience. St. Chrysostom writes that God is always waiting to hear our prayers, and that a case never occurred when he neglected to hear a petition offered to him properly: "God is always prepared for the voice of his servants, nor did he ever, when called upon as he ought to be, neglect to hear."[76] And in another place he says that when we pray to God, before we have finished recounting to him our supplications, he has already heard us: "It is always obtained, even while we are yet praying." We even have the promise of God to do this: "As they are yet speaking, I will hear" (Isaiah 65:24). The Lord, says David, stands near to everyone who prays, to console, to hear, and to save him: "The Lord is nigh to all them that call upon him; to all that call upon him in truth [that is, as they ought to call], he will do the will of them that fear him; and he will hear their prayer and will save them" (Psalm 145:18). This it was in which Moses gloried when he said, "There is not another nation so great that has gods so near them, as our God is present to all our petitions" (Deuteronomy 4:7). The gods of the Gentiles were deaf to those who invoked them, for they were wretched fabrications which could do nothing. But our God, who is Almighty, is not deaf to our prayers but always stands near the man who prays, ready to grant him all the graces which he asks: "In whatever day I shall call upon you, behold I shall know that you are my God" (Psalm 56:10). Lord, says the Psalmist, hereby do I know that you, my God, are all goodness and mercy: in that whenever I have recourse to you, you instantly help me.

---

76. *In Matt. hom. 55.*

IV.   We should not limit ourselves to asking for little things. To pray is better than to meditate.

We are so poor that we have nothing; but if we pray, we are no longer poor. If we are poor, God is rich; and God, as the Apostle says, is all liberality to him that calls for his aid: "Rich unto all who call upon him" (Romans 10:12) Since, therefore (as St. Augustine exhorts us), we have to do with a Lord of infinite power and infinite riches, let us not go to him for little and valueless things, but let us ask some great thing of him: "You seek from the Almighty; seek something great."[77] If a man went to a king to ask some trumpery coin, like a farthing, methinks that man would but insult his king. On the other hand we honor God, we honor his mercy and his liberality, when, though we see how miserable we are and how unworthy of any kindness, we yet ask for great graces, trusting in the goodness of God and in his faithfulness to his promises of granting to the man who prays whatever grace he asks: "Whatsoever you will, ask, and it shall be done unto you" (John 15:7). St. Mary Magdalene of Pazzi said: "God feels himself so honored and is so delighted when we ask for his grace that he is, in a certain sense, grateful to us, because when we do this we seem to open to him a way to do us a kindness and to satisfy his nature, which is to do good to all." And let us be sure that, when we seek God's grace, he always gives us more than we ask: "If any of you want wisdom, let him ask of God, who gives to all abundantly and upbraids not" (James 1:5). Thus speaks St. James to show us that God is not like men, parsimonious of his goods. Men, though rich and liberal, when they give alms are always somewhat close-handed and generally give less than is asked of them, because their wealth, however great it is, is always finite, so that the more they give, the less they have. But God, when he is asked, gives his good things "abundantly"—that is, with a generous hand, always giving more than is asked, because his wealth is infinite, and the more he gives, the more he has to give: "For you, O Lord, are sweet and mild, and plenteous in mercy to all who call upon you" (Psalm 86:5). You, O my God, said David, are but too liberal and kind to him who invokes you; the mercies which you pour upon him are superabundant, above all he asks.

---

77.   *In Ps.* 62.

On this point, then, we have to fix all our attention, namely, to pray with confidence, feeling sure that by prayer all the treasures of heaven are thrown open to us. "Let us attend to this," says St. Chrysostom, "and we shall open heaven to ourselves."[78] Prayer is a treasure; he who prays most receives most. St. Bonaventure says that every time a man has recourse to God by fervent prayer, he gains good things that are of more value than the whole world: "Any day a man gains more by devout prayer than the whole world is worth."[79] Some devout souls spend a great deal of time in reading and in meditating, but pay but little attention to prayer. There is no doubt that spiritual reading and meditation on the eternal truths are very useful things. "But," says St. Augustine, "it is of much more use to pray." By reading and meditating we learn our duty, but by prayer we obtain the grace to do it. "It is better to pray than to read: by reading we know what we ought to do; by prayer we receive what we ask." What is the use of knowing our duty and then not doing it, but to make us more guilty in God's sight? Read and meditate as we like, we shall never satisfy our obligations unless we ask of God the grace to fulfill them.

And, therefore, as St. Isidore observes, the devil is never more busy to distract us with the thoughts of worldly cares than when he perceives us praying and asking God for grace: "Then mostly does the devil insinuate thoughts, when he sees a man praying."[80] And why? Because the enemy sees that at no other time do we gain so many treasures of heavenly goods as when we pray. This is the chief fruit of mental prayer, to ask God for the graces which we need for perseverance and for eternal salvation; and chiefly for this reason it is that mental prayer is morally necessary for the soul, to enable it to preserve itself in the grace of God. For if a person does not remember in the time of meditation to ask for the help necessary for perseverance, he will not do so at any other time; for without meditation he will not think of asking for it and will not even think of the necessity for asking it. On the other hand, he who makes his meditation every day will easily see the needs of his soul, its dangers, and the necessity of his prayer; and so he will pray and will obtain the graces which will enable him to persevere and save his soul. Father Segneri said of himself

78. *In Act. hom.* 36.
79. *De Perf. vitae*, c. 5.
80. *Sent.*, book 3, c. 7.

that when he began to meditate, he aimed rather at exciting affections than at making prayers. But when he came to know the necessity and the immense utility of prayer, he more and more applied himself, in his long mental prayer, to making petitions.

"As a young swallow, so will I cry," said the devout king Hezekiah (Isaiah 38:14). The young of the swallow does nothing but cry to its mother for help and for food; so should we all do if we would preserve our life of grace. We should be always crying to God for aid to avoid the death of sin and to advance in his holy love. Father Rodriguez relates that the ancient Fathers, who were our first instructors in the spiritual life, held a conference to determine which was the exercise most useful and most necessary for eternal salvation; and that they determined it was to repeat over and over again the short prayer of David, "Incline unto my aid, O God!" (Psalm 70:2). "This," says Cassian, "is what everyone ought to do who wishes to be saved: he ought to be always saying, 'My God, help me! My God, help me!'" We ought to do this the first thing when we awake in the morning and then to continue doing it in all our needs and when attending to our business, whether spiritual or temporal, and most especially when we find ourselves troubled by any temptation or passion. St. Bonaventure says that at times we obtain a grace by a short prayer sooner than by many other good works: "Sometimes a man can sooner obtain by a short prayer what he would be a long time obtaining by pious works."[81] St. Ambrose says that he who prays, while he is praying obtains what he asks, because the very act of prayer is the same as receiving: "He who asks of God, while he asks receives; for to ask is to receive." Hence St. Chrysostom wrote, "There is nothing more powerful than a man who prays,"[82] because such a one is made partaker of the power of God. To arrive at perfection, says St. Bernard, we must meditate and pray: by meditation we see what we want; by prayer we receive what we want. "Let us mount by meditation and prayer: the one teaches what is deficient, the other obtains that there should be nothing deficient."[83]

---

81. *De Prof. Rel.*, book 2, c. 65.
82. *In Matt. hom.* 58.
83. *De S. And.*, s. 1.

Conclusion of the chapter

In conclusion, to save one's soul without prayer is most difficult and even (as we have seen) impossible, according to the ordinary course of God's Providence. But by praying our salvation is made secure and very easy. It is not necessary in order to save our souls to go among the heathen and give up our life. It is not necessary to retire into the desert and eat nothing but herbs. What does it cost us to say, "My God, help me! Lord, assist me! Have mercy on me!" Is there anything more easy than this? And this little will suffice to save us if we will be diligent in doing it. St. Laurence Justinian specially exhorts us to oblige ourselves to say a prayer at least when we begin any action: "We must endeavor to offer a prayer at least in the beginning of every work."[84] Cassian attests that the principal advice of the ancient Fathers was to have recourse to God with short but frequent prayers. Let no one, says St. Bernard, think lightly of prayer, because God values it and then gives us either what we ask, or what is still more useful to us: "Let no one undervalue his prayer, for God does not undervalue it. . . . He will give either what we ask, or what he knows to be better."[85] And let us understand that if we do not pray we have no excuse, because the grace of prayer is given to everyone. It is in our power to pray whenever we will, as David says of himself: "With me is prayer to the God of my life; I will say to God, 'You are my support'" (Psalm 42:9–10). On this point I shall speak at length in the second part, where I will make it quite clear that God gives to all the grace of prayer, in order that thereby they may obtain every help and even more than they need for keeping the divine law and for persevering till death. At present, I will only say that if we are not saved, the whole fault will be ours; and we shall have our own failure to answer for because we did not pray.

---

84. *Lign. vitae de or.*, c. 6.
85. *De Quad.*, s. 5.

CHAPTER III

The Conditions of Prayer

I. Which are the requisite conditions?

OBJECT OF PRAYER

"Amen, amen, I say to you, if you ask the Father anything in my name, he will give it you" (John 16:23). Jesus Christ, then, has promised that whatever we ask his Father in his name, his Father will give us—but always with the understanding that we ask under the proper conditions. Many seek, says St. James, and do not obtain because they seek improperly: "You ask and do not receive, because you ask amiss" (James 4:3). So St. Basil, following out the argument of the Apostle, says, "You sometimes ask and do not receive because you have asked badly; either without faith, or you have requested things not fit for you, or you have not persevered"[86]— "faithlessly," that is, with little faith, or little confidence; "lightly," with little desire of the grace you ask; "things not fit for you," when you seek good things that will not be conducive to your salvation; or you have left off praying, without perseverance. Hence St. Thomas reduces to four the conditions required in prayer in order that it may produce its effect. These are that a man asks (1) for himself; (2) things necessary for salvation; (3) piously; and (4) with perseverance.[87]

CAN WE PRAY EFFICACIOUSLY FOR OTHERS?

The first condition, then, of prayer is that you make it for yourself, because St. Thomas holds that one man cannot *ex condigno* (i.e., in the fitness of things) obtain for another eternal life; nor, consequently, even

---

86. *Const. Mon.*, c. 1.
87. *Summa* 2. 2. q. 83, a. 15.

those graces which are requisite for his salvation. Since, as he says, the promise is made not to others, but only to those that pray: "He shall give to you." Nevertheless, there are many theologians—Cornelius à Lapide, Sylvester, Tolet, Habert, and others—who hold the opposite doctrine on the authority of St. Basil, who teaches that prayer, by virtue of God's promise, is infallibly efficacious, even for those for whom we pray, provided they put no positive impediment in the way. And they support their doctrine by Scripture: "Pray one for another, that you may be saved; for the continual prayer of the just man avails much" (James 5:16). "Pray for them that persecute and slander you" (Luke 6:28). And better still, on the text of St. John: "He who knows his brother to sin a sin which is not to death, let him ask, and life shall be given to him who sins not unto death. There is a sin unto death; for that I say not that any man ask" (1 John 5:16). St. Ambrose, St. Augustine, the Ven. Bede, and others explain the words "who sins not unto death" to mean provided the sinner is not one who intends to remain obstinate till death; since for such a one, a very extraordinary grace would be required. But for other sinners, who are not guilty of such malice, the Apostle promises their conversion to him who prays for them: "Let him ask, and life shall be given him for him who sins."

WE OUGHT TO PRAY FOR SINNERS

Besides, it is quite certain that the prayers of others are of great use to sinners and are very pleasing to God; and God complains of his servants who do not recommend sinners to him, as he once complained to St. Mary Magdalene of Pazzi, to whom he said one day: "See, my daughter, how the Christians are in the devil's hands; if my elect did not deliver them by their prayers, they would be devoured." But God especially requires this of priests and religious. The same saint used to say to her nuns: "My sisters, God has not separated us from the world that we should only do good for ourselves, but also that we should appease him in behalf of sinners." And God one day said to her, "I have given to you my chosen spouses the City of Refuge (i.e., the Passion of Jesus Christ) so that you may have a place where you may obtain help for my creatures. Therefore have recourse to it, and thence stretch forth a helping hand to my creatures who are perishing, and lay down your lives for them." For this reason the saint, inflamed with holy zeal, used to offer God the blood of the Redeemer fifty times a day in behalf of sinners and was quite wasted away for the desire she had for their conversion. "Oh," she used to say, "what pain is it, O Lord, to see how one could help your creatures by giving one's life for them, and not be able to do so!" For the rest, in every exercise she recommended sinners to God; and it is written in her life that she scarcely passed an hour in the day without praying for them. Frequently, too, she arose in the middle of the night and went to the Blessed Sacrament to pray for them; and yet for all this, when she was once found bathed in tears, on being asked the cause, she answered, "Because I seem to myself to do nothing for the salvation of sinners." She went so far as to offer to endure even the pains of hell for their conversion, provided that in that place she might still love God; and often God gratified her by inflicting on her grievous pains and infirmities for the salvation of sinners. She prayed especially for priests, seeing that their good life was the occasion of salvation to others, while their bad life was the cause of ruin to many; and therefore she prayed God to visit their faults upon her, saying, "Lord, make me die and return to life again as many times as is necessary to satisfy your justice for them!" And it is related in her life that the saint, by her prayers, did indeed release many souls from the hands of Lucifer.

I wished to speak rather particularly of the zeal of this saint; but, indeed, no souls who really love God neglect to pray for poor sinners. For how is it possible for a person who loves God, and knows what love he has for our souls, and what Jesus Christ has done and suffered for their salvation, and how our Savior desires us to pray for sinners—how is it possible, I say, that he should be able to look with indifference on the numbers of poor souls who are living without God and are slaves of hell, without being moved to importune God with frequent prayers to give light and strength to these wretched beings, so that they may come out from the miserable state of living death in which they are slumbering? True it is that God has not promised to grant our requests when those for whom we pray put a positive impediment in the way of their conversion. But still, God of his goodness has often deigned, at the prayer of his servants, to bring back the most blinded and obstinate sinners to a state of salvation, by means of extraordinary graces. Therefore let us never omit, when we say or hear Mass, when we receive Holy Communion, when we make our meditation or our visit to the Blessed Sacrament, to recommend poor sinners to God. And a learned author says that he who prays for others will find that his prayers for himself are heard much sooner. But this is a digression. Let us now return to the examination of the other conditions that St. Thomas lays down as necessary to the efficacy of prayer.

WE MUST ASK FOR GRACES NECESSARY TO SALVATION

The second condition assigned by the saint is that we ask those favors which are necessary to salvation, because the promise annexed to prayer was not made with reference to temporal favors, which are not necessary for the salvation of the soul. St. Augustine, explaining the words of the Gospel "whatever you shall ask in my name," says that "nothing which is asked in a way detrimental to salvation is asked in the name of the Savior."[88] Sometimes, says the same Father, we seek some temporal favors, and God does not hear us; but he does not hear us because he loves us and wishes to be merciful to us. "A man may pray faithfully for the necessities of this life, and God may mercifully refuse to hear him because the physician knows better than the patient what is good for the sick man."[89] The physician who loves his patient will not allow him to have those things that he sees would do him harm. Oh, how many, if they had been sick or poor, would have escaped those sins which they commit in health and in affluence! And, therefore, when men ask God for health or riches, he often denies them because he loves them, knowing that these things would be to them an occasion of losing his grace, or at any rate of growing tepid in the spiritual life. Not that we mean to say that it is any defect to pray to God for the necessaries of this present life, so far as they are not inconsistent with our eternal salvation, as the wise man said: "Give me only the necessaries of life" (Proverbs 30:8). Nor is it a defect, says St. Thomas,[90] to have anxiety about such goods,

88. *In Jo. tr.* 102.
89. *Ap. s. Prosp. Sent.*, 212.
90. *Summa*, 2.2, q. 83, a. 6.

if it is not inordinate. The defect consists in desiring and seeking these temporal goods, and in having an inordinate anxiety about them, as if they were our highest good. Therefore, when we ask of God these temporal favors, we ought always to ask them with resignation and with the condition, if they will be useful to our souls; and when we see that God does not grant them, let us be certain that he then denies them to us for the love he bears us, and because he sees that they would be injurious to the salvation of our souls.

It often happens that we pray God to deliver us from some dangerous temptation, and yet that God does not hear us but permits the temptation to continue troubling us. In such a case, let us understand that God permits even this for our greater good. It is not temptation or bad thoughts that separate us from God, but our consent to the evil. When a soul in temptation recommends itself to God, and by his aid resists, oh, how it then advances in perfection and unites itself more closely to God! And this is the reason why God does not hear it. St. Paul prayed instantly to be delivered from the temptation of impurity: "There was given me a sting of my flesh, an angel of Satan to buffet me; for which thing thrice I besought the Lord that it might depart from me" (2 Corinthians 12:7). But God answered him that it was enough to have his grace: "My grace is sufficient for you." So that even in temptations we ought to pray with resignation, saying, "Lord, deliver me from this trouble, if it is expedient to deliver me; and if not, at least give me help to resist." And here comes in what St. Bernard says, that when we beg any grace of God, he gives us either that which we ask or some other thing more useful to us. He often leaves us to be buffeted by the waves in order to try our faithfulness and for our greater profit. It seems then that he is deaf to our prayers. But no; let us be sure that God then really hears us and secretly aids us, and strengthens us by his grace to resist all the assaults of our enemies. See how he himself assures us of this by the mouth of the Psalmist: "You called upon me in affliction, and I delivered you; I heard you in the secret place of tempest; I proved you at the waters of contradiction" (Psalm 81:8).

Chapter III

OTHER CONDITIONS OF PRAYER

The other conditions assigned by St. Thomas to prayer are that it is to be made piously and perseveringly. By piously, he means with humility and confidence; by perseveringly, continuing to pray until death. We must now speak distinctly of each of these three conditions, which are the most necessary for prayer, namely, of humility, confidence, and perseverance.

II. The humility with which we should pray

The Lord does indeed regard the prayers of his servants, but only of his servants who are humble. "He has had regard to the prayer of the humble?" (Psalm 102:18). Others he does not regard but rejects them: "God resists the proud and gives grace to the humble" (James 4:6). He does not hear the prayers of the proud, who trust in their own strength, but for that reason leaves them to their own feebleness; and in this state, deprived of God's aid, they must certainly perish. David had to bewail this case: "Before I was humbled, I offended" (Psalm 119:67). I sinned because I was not humble. The same thing happened to St. Peter, who, though he was warned by our Lord that all the disciples would abandon him on that night—"All you shall be scandalized in me this night" (Matthew 26:31)—nevertheless, instead of acknowledging his own weakness and begging our Lord's aid against his unfaithfulness, was too confident in his own strength and said that, though all should abandon him, he would never leave him: "Although all shall be scandalized in you, I will never be scandalized." And although our Savior again foretold to him in a special manner that, in that very night, before the cock-crow, he should deny him three times, yet, trusting in his own courage, he boasted, saying, "Yes, though I should die with you, I will not deny you." But what came of it? Scarcely had the unhappy man entered the house of the high priest, when he was accused of being a disciple of Jesus Christ and three times did he deny with an oath that he had ever known him. And again, he denied with an oath, "I know not the Man." If Peter had humbled himself and had asked our Lord for the grace of constancy, he would not have denied him.

We ought all to feel that we are standing on the edge of a precipice, suspended over the abyss of all sins, and supported only by the thread of God's grace. If this thread fails us, we shall certainly fall into the gulf and shall commit the most horrible wickedness. "Unless the Lord had been my helper, my soul would have almost dwelt in hell" (Psalm 94:17). If God had not succored me, I would have fallen into a thousand sins, and now I would be in hell. So said the Psalmist, and so ought each of us to say. This is what St. Francis of Assisi meant when he said that he was the worst sinner in the world. But, my Father, said his companion, what you say is not true; there are many in the world who are certainly worse than you are. Yes, what I say is but too true, answered St. Francis, because if God did not keep his hand over me, I should commit every possible sin.

It is of faith that without the aid of grace we cannot do any good work, nor even think a good thought. "Without grace men do no good whatever, either in thought or in deed," says St. Augustine.[91] As the eye cannot see without light, so, say the holy Father, man can do no good without grace. The Apostle had said the same thing before him: "Not that we are sufficient to think anything of ourselves, as of ourselves; but our sufficiency is of God" (2 Corinthians 3:5). And David had said it before St. Paul: "Unless the Lord builds the house, they labor in vain who build it" (Psalm 127:1). In vain does man weary himself to become a saint unless God lends a helping hand: "Unless the Lord keeps the city, he watches in vain who keeps it." If God did not preserve the soul from sins, in vain will it try to preserve itself by its own strength. And therefore did the holy prophet protest, "I will not trust in my bow" (Psalm 44:7). I will not hope in my arms, but only in God, who alone can save me.

Hence, whoever finds that he has done any good and does not find that he has fallen into greater sins than those which are commonly committed, let him say with St. Paul, "By the grace of God I am what I am" (1 Corinthians 15:10). And for the same reason, he ought never to cease to be afraid of falling on every occasion of sin: "Wherefore, he who thinks himself to stand, let him take heed lest he fall" (1 Corinthians 10:12). St. Paul wishes to warn us that he who feels secure of not falling is in great

---

91. *De Corr. et Gr.*, c. 2.

danger of falling; and he assigns the reason in another place, where he says, "If any man thinks himself to be something, whereas he is nothing, he deceives himself" (Galatians 6:3). So that St. Augustine wrote wisely, "The presumption of stability renders many unstable; no one will be so firm as he who feels himself infirm."[92] If a man says he has no fear, it is a sign that he trusts in himself and in his good resolutions; but such a man, with his mischievous confidence, deceives himself because through trust in his own strength, he neglects to fear; and through not fearing, he neglects to recommend himself to God, and then he will certainly fall. And so, for like reasons, we should all abstain from noticing with any vainglory the sins of other people; but rather we should then esteem ourselves as worse in ourselves than they are, and should say, "Lord, if you had not helped me, I would have done worse." Otherwise, to punish us for our pride, God will permit us to fall into worse and more shameful sins. For this cause St. Paul instructs us to labor for our salvation. But how? Always in fear and trembling: "With fear and trembling work out your salvation" (Philippians 2:12) Yes; for he who has a great fear of falling distrusts his own strength and therefore places his confidence in God and will have recourse to him in dangers. And God will aid him, and so he will vanquish his temptations and will be saved. St. Philip Neri, walking one day through Rome, kept saying, "I am in despair!" A certain religious rebuked him, and the saint thereupon said, "My father, I am in despair for myself; but I trust in God." So must we do if we would be saved; we must always live in despair of doing anything by our own strength; and in so doing we shall imitate St. Philip, who used to say to God the first moment he woke in the morning, "Lord, keep your hands over Philip this day; for if not, Philip will betray you." This, then, we may conclude with St. Augustine, is all the grand science of a Christian: to know that he is nothing and can do nothing. "This is the whole of the great science, to know that man is nothing."[93] For then he will never neglect to furnish himself, by prayer to God, with that strength which he has not of himself, and which he needs in order to resist temptation and to do good; and so, with the help of God, who never refuses anything to the man who prays to

---

92.   Serm. 76, E. B.
93.   *In Ps.* 70., s.1.

him in humility, he will be able to do all things: "The prayer of him who humbles himself shall pierce the clouds, and he will not depart until the Most High beholds" (Sirach 35:17). The prayer of a humble soul penetrates the heavens and presents itself before the throne of God and departs not without God's looking on it and hearing it. And though the soul is guilty of any amount of sin, God never despises a heart that humbles itself: "A contrite and humble heart, O God, you will not despise" (Psalm 51:19); "God resists the proud but gives grace to the humble" (James 4:6). As the Lord is severe with the proud and resists their prayers, so is he kind and liberal to the humble. This is precisely what Jesus Christ said one day to St. Catherine of Sienna: "Know, my daughter that a soul who perseveres in humble prayer gains every virtue."[94]

It will be of use to introduce here the advice which the learned and pious Palafox, Bishop of Osma, gives to spiritual persons who desire to become saints. It occurs in a note to the eighteenth letter of St. Teresa, which she wrote to her confessor to give him an account of all the grades of supernatural prayer with which God had favored her. On this the bishop writes that these supernatural graces which God designed to grant to St. Teresa, as he has also done to other saints, are not necessary in order to arrive at sanctity, since many souls have become saints without them; and, on the other hand, many have arrived at sanctity and yet have, after all, been damned. Therefore he says it is superfluous, and even presumptuous, to desire and to ask for these supernatural gifts, when the true and only way to be come a saint is to exercise ourselves in virtue and in the love of God; and this is done by means of prayer and by corresponding to the inspirations and assistance of God, who wishes nothing so much as to see us saints, "For this is the will of God, your sanctification" (1 Thessalonians 4:3).

Hence Bishop Palafox, speaking of the grades of supernatural prayer mentioned in St. Teresa's letter, namely, the prayer of quiet, the sleep or suspension of the faculties, the prayer of union, ecstasy, or rapture, flight and impulse of the spirit, and the wound of love, says very wisely that as regards the prayer of quiet, what we ought to ask of God is that he would free us from attachment to worldly goods and the desire of them,

94. *Ap. Blos. in Concl.*, p. 2, c. 3.

which give no peace but bring disquiet and affliction to the soul: "Vanity of vanities" (Ecclesiastes 1:2), as Solomon well called them, and vexation of spirit. The heart of man will never find true peace if it does not empty itself of all that is not God, so as to leave itself all free for his love that he alone may possess the whole of it. But this the soul cannot do of itself; it must obtain it of God by repeated prayers. As regards the sleep and suspension of the faculties, we ought to ask God for grace to keep them asleep for all that is temporal and only awake them to consider God's goodness and to set our hearts upon his love and eternal happiness. As regards the union of the faculties, let us pray him to give us grace not to think, nor to seek, nor to wish anything but what God wills; since all sanctity and the perfection of love consists in uniting our will to the will of God. As regards ecstasy and rapture, let us pray God to draw us away from the inordinate love of ourselves and of creatures, and to draw us entirely to himself. As regards the flight of the spirit, let us pray him to give us grace to live altogether detached from this world, and to do as the swallows that do not settle on the ground even to feed, but take their food flying; so should we use our temporal goods for all that is necessary for the support of life, but always flying, without settling on the ground to look for earthly pleasures, As regards impulse of spirit, let us pray him to give us courage and strength to do violence to ourselves, whenever it is necessary, for resisting the assaults of our enemies, for conquering our passions, and for accepting sufferings even in the midst of desolation and dryness of spirit. Finally, as regards the wound of love, as a wound by its pain perpetually renews the remembrance of what we suffer, so ought we to pray God to wound our hearts with his holy love in such a way that we shall always be reminded of his goodness and the love which he has borne us; and thus we should live in continual love of him and should be always pleasing him with our works and our affections. But none of these graces can be obtained without prayer; and with prayer, provided it is humble, confident, and persevering, everything is obtained.

III.   The confidence with which we ought to pray

EXCELLENCE AND NECESSITY OF THIS VIRTUE

The principal instruction that St. James gives us, if we wish by prayer to obtain grace from God, is that we pray with a confidence that feels sure of being heard, and without hesitating: "Let him ask in faith, nothing wavering" (James 1:6). St. Thomas teaches that, as prayer receives its power of meriting from charity, so on the other hand it receives from faith and confidence its power of being efficacious to obtain: "Prayer has its power of meriting from charity, but its efficacy of obtaining from faith and confidence."[95] St. Bernard teaches the same, saying that it is our confidence alone which obtains for us the divine mercies: "Hope alone obtains a place of mercy with you, O Lord."[96] God is much pleased with our confidence in his mercy because we then honor and exalt that infinite goodness which it was his object in creating us to manifest to the world: "Let all those, O my God," says the royal prophet, "who hope in you be glad, for they shall be eternally happy, and you shall dwell in them" (Psalm 5:12). God protects and saves all those who confide in him: "He is the Protector of all that hope in him" (Psalm 18:31). "You who save them that trust in you" (Psalm 17:7). Oh, the great promises that are recorded in the Scriptures to all those who hope in God! He who hopes in God will not fall into sin: "None of them that trust in him shall offend" (Psalm 34:23). Yes, says David, because God has his eyes turned to all those who confide in his goodness to deliver them by his aid from the death of sin. "Behold, the eyes of the Lord are on them that fear him, and on them that hope for his mercy to deliver their souls from death" (Psalm 33:18–19). And in another place God himself says, "Because he hoped in me I will deliver him; I will protect him; I will deliver him, and I will glorify him" (Psalm 91:14). Mark the word "because." Because he confided in me, I will protect, I will deliver him from his enemies and from the danger of falling, and finally I will give him eternal glory. Isaiah says of those who place their hope in God, "They that hope in the Lord shall renew their strength; they shall take wings as the eagles; they shall run and not be weary; they shall walk and not faint" (Isaiah 40:31). They shall cease

95.   *Summa*, 2.2, q. 83, a. 15.
96.   *De Annunt.*, s. 3.

to be weak as they are now and shall gain in God a great strength; they shall not faint; they shall not even feel weary in walking the way of salvation, but they shall run and fly as eagles. "In silence and in hope shall your strength be" (Isaiah 30:15). All our strength, the prophet tells us, consists in placing all our confidence in God and in being silent—that is, in reposing in the arms of his mercy, without trusting to our own efforts or to human means.

And when did it ever happen that a man had confidence in God and was lost? "No one has hoped in the Lord and has been confounded" (Sirach 2:10). It was this confidence that assured David that he should not perish: "In you, O Lord, have I trusted; I shall not be confounded forever" (Psalm 31:2). Perhaps, then, says St. Augustine, could God be a deceiver, who offers to support us in dangers if we lean upon him and would then withdraw himself if we had recourse to him? "God is not a deceiver that he should offer to support us, and then when we lean upon him should slip away from us."[97] David calls the man happy who trusts in God: "Blessed is the man who trust in you" (Psalm 84:13). And why? Because, says he, he who trusts in God will always find himself surrounded by God's mercy. "Mercy shall encompass him who hopes in the Lord" (Psalm 32:10). So that he shall be surrounded and guarded by God on every side in such a way that he shall be prevented from losing his soul.

It is for this cause that the Apostle recommends us so earnestly to preserve our confidence in God; for (he tells us) it will certainly obtain from him a great remuneration: "Do not therefore lose your confidence, which has a great reward" (Hebrews 10:35). As is our confidence, so shall be the graces we receive from God. If our confidence is great, great too will be the graces: "Great faith merits great things."[98] St. Bernard writes that the divine mercy is an inexhaustible fountain, and that he who brings to it the largest vessel of confidence shall take from it the largest measure of gifts: "Neither, O Lord, do you put the oil of your mercy into any other vessel than that of confidence."[99] The Prophet had long before expressed the same thought: "Let your mercy, O Lord, be upon

97. *S. Thomas. Erud. Princ.*, book 2, c. 5.
98. *In Cant.*, s. 32.
99. *De Annunt.*, s. 3.

us (i.e., in proportion) as we have hoped in you" (Psalm 33:22). This was well exemplified in the centurion to whom our Savior said, in praise of his confidence, "Go, and as you have believed, so be it done unto you" (Matthew 8:31). And our Lord revealed to St. Gertrude that he who prays with confidence does him, in a manner, such violence that he cannot but hear him in everything he asks: "Prayer," says St. John Climacus, "does a pious violence to God." It does him a violence, but a violence which he likes, and which pleases him.

"Let us go, therefore," according to the admonition of St. Paul, "with confidence to the throne of grace, so that we may obtain mercy and find grace in seasonable aid" (Hebrews 4:16). The throne of grace is Jesus Christ, who is now sitting on the right hand of the Father—not on the throne of justice, but of grace, to obtain pardon for us if we fall into sin, and help to enable us to persevere if we are enjoying his friendship. To this throne we must always have recourse with confidence; that is to say, with that trust which springs from faith in the goodness and truth of God, who has promised to hear him who prays to him with confidence, but with a confidence that is both sure and stable. On the other hand, says St. James, do not let the man who prays with hesitation think that he will receive anything: "For he who wavers is like a wave of the sea, which is moved and carried about by the wind. Therefore let not that man think to receive anything of the Lord" (James 1:6). He will receive nothing, because the diffidence which agitates him is unjust toward God and will hinder his mercy from listening to his prayers: "You have not asked rightly, because you have asked doubtingly," says St. Basil; "you have not received grace, because you have asked it without confidence."[100] David says that our confidence in God ought to be as firm as a mountain, which is not moved by each gust of wind. "They who trust in the Lord are as Mount Zion; he shall not be moved forever" (Psalm 125:1). And it is this that our Lord recommends to us if we wish to obtain the graces which we ask: "Whatsoever you ask when you pray, believe that you shall receive, and they shall come unto you" (Marl 11:24). Whatever grace you require, be sure of having it, and so you shall obtain it.

---

100. *Const. Mon.*, c. 2.

FOUNDATION OF OUR CONFIDENCE

But on what, a man will say, am I, a miserable sinner, to found this certain confidence of obtaining what I ask? On what? On the promise made by Jesus Christ: "Ask, and you shall receive" (John 16:24) "Who will fear to be deceived, when the truth promises ?" says St. Augustine.[101] How can we doubt that we shall be heard, when God, who is truth itself, promises to give us that which we ask of him in prayer? "We should not be exhorted to ask," says the same Father, "unless he meant to give."[102] Certainly God would not have exhorted us to ask him for favors if he had not determined to grant them; but this is the very thing to which he exhorts us so strongly, and which is repeated so often in the Scriptures—pray, ask, seek, and you shall obtain what you desire: "Whatever you will, seek and it shall be done to you" (John 15:7). And in order that we may pray to him with due confidence, our Savior has taught us, in the Our Father, that when we have recourse to him for the graces necessary to salvation (all of which are included in the petitions of the Lord's Prayer) we should call him not Lord, but Father—"Our Father"—because it is his will that we should ask God for grace with the same confidence with which a son, when in want or sick, asks food or medicine from his own father. If a son is dying of hunger, he has only to make his case known to his father, and his father will forthwith provide him with food; and if he has received a bite from a venomous serpent, he has only to show his father the wound, and the father will immediately apply whatever remedy he has.

Trusting, therefore, in God's promises, let us always pray with confidence—not vacillating, but stable and firm, as the Apostle says: "Let us hold fast the confession of our hope without wavering; for he is faithful that has promised" (Hebrews 10:23). As it is perfectly certain that God is faithful in his promises, so ought our faith also to be perfectly certain that he will hear us when we pray. And although sometimes, when we are in a state of aridity or disturbed by some fault we have committed, we perhaps do not feel while praying that sensible confidence which we would wish to experience, yet, for all this, let us force ourselves to pray and to pray without ceasing; for God will not neglect to hear us. No,

---

101. *Confessions*, book 12, c. 1.
102. Serm. 105, E. B.

rather he will hear us more readily; because we shall then pray with more distrust of ourselves, and confiding only in the goodness and faithfulness of God, who has promised to hear the man who prays to him. Oh, how God is pleased in the time of our tribulations, of our fears, and of our temptations to see us hope against hope—that is, in spite of the feeling of diffidence which we then experience because of our desolation! This is that for which the Apostle praises the patriarch Abraham, "who against hope, believed in hope" (Romans 4:18).

St. John says that he who reposes a sure trust in God certainly will become a saint: "And everyone who has this hope in him sanctifies himself, as he also is holy" (1 John 3:3). For God gives abundant graces to them who trust in him. By this confidence the host of martyrs, of virgins, even of children, in spite of the dread of the torments which their persecutors prepared for them, overcame both their tortures and their persecutors. Sometimes, I say, we pray, but it seems to us that God will not hear us. Alas! Let us not then neglect to persevere in prayer and in hope; let us then say, with Job, "Although he should kill me, I will trust in him" (Job 13:15). O my God! Though you have driven me from your presence, I will not cease to pray and to hope in your mercy. Let us do so, and we shall obtain what we want from God. So did the Canaanite woman, and she obtained all that she wished from Jesus Christ. This woman had a daughter possessed by a devil and prayed our Savior to deliver her: "Have mercy on me; my daughter is grievously tormented by a devil" (Matthew 15:22). Our Lord answered her that he was not sent for the Gentiles, of whom she was one, but for the Jews. She, however, did not lose heart, but renewed her prayer with confidence: Lord, you can console me! You must console me: "Lord, help me!" Jesus answered, But as to the bread of the children, it is not good to give it to the dogs: "It is not good to take the children's bread and to cast it to the dogs" But, my Lord, she answered, even the dogs are allowed to have the fragments of bread which fall from the table: "Yes, Lord; for the whelps eat of the crumbs that fall from the tables of their masters." Then our Savior, seeing the great confidence of this woman, praised her and did what she asked, saying: "O woman, great is your faith; be it done to you as you will." For who, says Sirach, has ever called on God for aid and has been neglected and left unaided by him? "Or who has called upon him, and he has despised him?" (Sirach 2:10).

St. Augustine says that prayer is a key which opens heaven to us; the same moment in which our prayer ascends to God, the grace which we ask for descends to us: "The prayer of the just is the key of heaven; the petition ascends, and the mercy of God descends."[103] The royal prophet writes that our supplications and God's mercy are united together: "Blessed is God, who has not turned away my prayer, nor his mercy for me" (Psalm 66:20). And hence the same St. Augustine says that when we are praying to God, we ought to be certain that God is hearing us: "When you see that your prayer is not removed from you, be sure that his mercy is not removed from you."[104] And for myself, I speak the truth, I never feel greater consolation, nor a greater confidence of my salvation, than when I am praying to God and recommending myself to him. And I think that the same thing happens to all other believers; for the other signs of our salvation are uncertain and unstable; but that God hears the man who prays to him with confidence is an infallible truth, as it is infallible that God cannot fail in his promises.

When we find ourselves weak and unable to overcome any passion or any great difficulty so as to fulfill that which God requires of us, let us take courage and say, with the Apostle, "I can do all things in him who strengthens me" (Philippians 4:13). Let us not say, as some do, "I cannot; I distrust myself." With our own strength certainly we can do nothing; but with God's help we can do everything. If God said to anyone, "Take this mountain on your back, and carry it, for I am helping you," would not the man be a mistrustful fool if he answered, "I will not take it; for I have not strength to carry it"? And thus, when we know how miserable and weak we are, and when we find ourselves most encompassed with temptations, let us not lose heart; but let us lift up our eyes to God and say, with David, "The Lord is my helper; and I will despise my enemies" (Psalm 118:7). With the help of my Lord, I shall overcome and laugh to scorn all the assaults of my foes. And when we find ourselves in danger of offending God or in any other critical position, and are too confused

---

103. Serm. 47, E. B. app.
104. *In Ps.* 65.

to know what is best to be done, let us recommend ourselves to God, saying, "The Lord is my light and my salvation; whom shall I fear" (Psalm 27:1). And let us be sure that God will then certainly give us light, and will save us from every evil.

THE PRAYER OF SINNERS

But I am a sinner, you will say, and in the Scriptures I read, "God does not hear sinners" (John 9:31). St. Thomas answers (with St. Augustine) that this was said by the blind man, who when he spoke had not as yet been enlightened: "That is the word of a blind man not yet perfectly enlightened, and therefore it is not authoritative."[105] Though, adds St. Thomas, it is true of the petition which the sinner makes, "so far forth as he is a sinner"—that is, when he asks from a desire of continuing to sin; as, for instance, if he were to ask assistance to enable him to take revenge on his enemy or to execute any other bad intention. The same holds good for the sinner who prays God to save him but has no desire to quit the state of sin. There are some unhappy persons who love the chains with which the devil keeps them bound like slaves. The prayers of such men are not heard by God because they are rash, presumptuous, and abominable. For what greater presumption can there be than for a man to ask favors of a prince whom he not only has of ten offended, but whom he intends to offend still more? And this is the meaning of the Holy Spirit when he says that the prayer of him who turns away his ears so as not to hear what God commands is detestable and odious to God: "He who turns away his ears from learning the law, his prayer shall be an abomination" (Proverbs 28:9). To these people God says, it is of no use your praying to me, for I will turn my eyes from you, and will not hear you: "When you stretch forth your hands, I will turn away my eyes from you; and when you multiply prayer, I will not hear" (Isaiah 1:15) Such, precisely, was the prayer of the impious King Antiochus, who prayed to God and made great promises, but insincerely and with a heart obstinate in sin, the sole object of his prayer being to escape the punishment that impended over him; therefore God did not hear his prayer but caused him to die devoured by worms: "Then this

---

105. *Summa*, 2.2, q. 83, a. 16.

wicked man prayed to the Lord, of whom he was not to obtain mercy"
(2 Maccabees 9:13).

But others, who sin through frailty or by the violence of some great
passion, and who groan under the yoke of the enemy, and desire to
break these chains of death, and to escape from their miserable slavery,
and therefore ask the assistance of God—the prayer of these, if it is
persevering, will certainly be heard by him, who says that everyone that
asks receives, and he who seeks grace finds it: "For everyone that asks
receives, and he who seeks finds" (Matthew 7:8)—"everyone, whether
he is a just man or a sinner," says the author of the *Opus Imperfectum*.[106]
And in St. Luke, our Lord, when speaking of the man who gave all the
loaves he had to his friend not so much on account of his friendship as
because of the other's importunity, says, "If he shall continue knocking, I say to you, although he will not rise and give him because he is
his friend, yet because of his importunity he will rise and give him as
many as he needs" (Luke 11:8). And so I say unto you, "Ask, and it shall
be given you." So that persevering prayer obtains mercy from God, even
for those who are not his friends. That which is not obtained through
friendship, says St. Chrysostom, is obtained by prayer: "That which was
not effected by friendship was effected by prayer." He even says that prayer
is valued more by God than friendship: "Friendship is not of such avail
with God as prayer; that which is not effected by friendship is effected
by prayer."[107] And St. Basil does not doubt that even sinners obtain what
they ask if they persevere in praying: "Sinners obtain what they seek, if
they seek perseveringly."[108] St. Gregory says the same: "The sinner also
shall cry, and his prayer shall reach to God."[109] So St. Jerome,[110] who says
that even the sinner can call God his Father if he prays to him to receive
him anew as a son, after the example of the Prodigal Son, who called him
Father—"Father, I have sinned" (Luke 15:21)—even though he had not
as yet been pardoned. If God did not hear sinners, says St. Augustine,
in vain would the Publican have asked for forgiveness: "If God does not

106. Hom. 18.
107. *Hom. Non esse desp.*
108. *Const. Mon.,* c. 1.
109. *In Ps. vi. paen.*
110. *Ep. ad Dam. de Fil. prod.*

hear sinners, in vain would that Publican have said, 'God be merciful to me, a sinner.'"[111] But the Gospel assures us that the Publican did by his prayer obtain forgiveness: "This man went down to his house justified" (Luke 18:14).

But further still, St. Thomas examines this point more minutely and does not hesitate to affirm that even the sinner is heard if he prays; for though his prayer is not meritorious, yet it has the power of impetration—that is, of obtaining what we ask—because impetration is not founded on God's justice but on his goodness. "Merit," he says, "depends on justice; impetration, on grace."[112] Thus did Daniel pray, "Incline, O my God, your ear and hear. . . . For not in our justifications do we present our prayers before your face, but in the multitude of your mercies" (Daniel 9:18). Therefore when we pray, says St. Thomas, it is not necessary to be friends of God in order to obtain the grace we ask; for prayer itself renders us his friends: "Prayer itself makes us of the family of God."[113] Moreover, St. Bernard uses a beautiful explanation of this, saying that the prayer of a sinner to escape from sin arises from the desire to return to the grace of God. Now this desire is a gift, which is certainly given by no other than God himself; to what end, therefore, says St. Bernard, would God give to a sinner this holy desire, unless he meant to hear him? "For what would he give the desire, unless he willed to hear?" And, indeed, in the Holy Scriptures themselves there are multitudes of instances of sinners who have been delivered from sin by prayer. Thus was King Ahab delivered (1 Kings 21:27); thus King Manasseh (2 Chronicles 33:12); thus King Nebuchadnezzar (Daniel 4:31); and thus the good thief (Luke 23:42). Oh, the wonderful, oh, the mighty power of prayer! Two sinners are dying on Calvary by the side of Jesus Christ: one, because he prays, "Remember me," is saved; the other, because he does not pray, is damned.

And finally St. Chrysostom says, "No man has with sorrow asked favors from him without obtaining what he wished."[114] No sinner has ever with penitence prayed to God without having his desires granted. But why should we cite more authorities, and give more reasons, to demonstrate

---

111. *In Jo. tr.* 44
112. *Summa*, 2.2, q. 83, a. 16.
113. *Comp. Theol.*, p. 2, c. 2.
114. *Hom. de Moys.*

this point when our Lord himself says, "Come to me, all you that labor and are burdened, and I will refresh you" (Matthew 11:28). The "burdened," according to Saints Augustine, Jerome, and others, are sinners in general, who groan under the load of their sins, and who, if they have recourse to God, will surely, according to his promise, be refreshed and saved by his grace. Ah, we cannot desire to be pardoned so much as he longs to pardon us. "You do not," says St. Chrysostom, "so much desire your sins to be forgiven, as he desires to forgive your sins."[115] There is no grace, he goes on to say, that is not obtained by prayer, though it be the prayer of the most abandoned sinner, provided only it be persevering: "There is nothing which prayer cannot obtain, though a man is guilty of a thousand sins, provided it is fervent and unremitting." And let us mark well the words of St. James: "If any man wants wisdom, let him ask of God, who gives to all abundantly and upbraids not" (James 1:5). All those, therefore, who pray to God, are infallibly heard by him and receive grace in abundance: "He gives to all abundantly." But you should particularly remark the words which follow, "and upbraids not." This means that God does not do as men, who, when a person who has formerly done them an injury comes to ask a favor, immediately upbraid him with his offense. God does not do so to the man who prays, even though he were the greatest sinner in the world, when he asks for some grace conducive to his eternal salvation. Then he does not upbraid him with the offenses he has committed; but, as though he had never displeased him, he instantly receives him, he consoles him, he hears him, and enriches him with an abundance of his gifts. To crown all, our Savior, in order to encourage us to pray, says, "Amen, amen, I say to you, if you ask the Father anything in my name, he will give it you" (John 16:23). As though he had said: "Courage, O sinners; do not despair; do not let your sins turn you away from having recourse to my Father, and from hoping to be saved by him, if you desire it. You have not now any merits to obtain the graces which you ask for, for you only deserve to be punished. Still, do this: go to my Father in my name, through my merits ask the favors which you want, and I promise and swear to you ('Amen, amen, I say to you,' which, according to St. Augustine, is a species of oath) that whatever you ask,

---

115. *In Act. hom.* 36.

my Father will grant." O God, what greater comfort can a sinner have after his fall than to know for certain that all that he asks from God in the name of Jesus Christ will be given to him!

I say "all," but I mean only that which has reference to his eternal salvation; for with respect to temporal goods, we have already shown that God, even when asked, sometimes does not give them because he sees that they would injure our soul. Bat so far as relates to spiritual goods, his promise to hear us is not conditional but absolute; and therefore St. Augustine tells us that those things which God promises absolutely, we should demand with absolute certainty of receiving: "Those things which God promises, seek with certainty."[116] And how, says the saint, can God ever deny us anything when we ask him for it with confidence? How much more does he desire to dispense to us his graces than we to receive them! "He is more willing to be munificent of his benefits to you than you are desirous to receive them."[117]

St. Chrysostom says that the only time when God is angry with us is when we neglect to ask him for his gifts: "He is only angry when we do not pray."[118] And how can it ever happen that God will not hear a soul who asks him for favors all according to his pleasure? When the soul says to him, Lord, I ask you not for goods of this world, riches, pleasures, honors; I ask you only for your grace: deliver me from sin, grant me a good death, give me Paradise, give me your holy love (which is that grace which St. Francis de Sales says we should seek more than all others), give me resignation to your will—how is it possible that God should not hear! What petitions will you, O my God, ever hear (says St. Augustine), if you do not hear those which are made after your own heart? "What prayers do you hear, if you do not hear not these?"[119] But, above all, our confidence ought to revive when we pray to God for spiritual graces, as Jesus Christ says: "If you, being evil, know how to give good gifts to your children, how much more will your Father from heaven give the good Spirit to them that ask him?" (Luke 11:15). If you, who are so attached to your own interests, so full of self-love, cannot refuse your children that

---

116. Serm. 354, E. B.
117. Serm. 105, E. B.
118. *In Matt.*, hom. 23.
119. *De Civ. Dei*, book 22, c. 8.

which they ask, how much more will your heavenly Father, who loves you better than any earthly father, grant you his spiritual goods when you pray for them!

IV. The perseverance required in prayer

Our prayers, then, must be humble and confident; but this is not enough to obtain final perseverance and thereby eternal life. Individual prayers will obtain the individual graces which they ask of God; but unless they are persevering, they will not obtain final perseverance: which, as it is the accumulation of many graces, requires many prayers that are not to cease till death. The grace of salvation is not a single grace but a chain of graces, all of which are at last linked with the grace of final perseverance. Now, to this chain of graces there ought to correspond another chain (as it were) of our prayers; if we, by neglecting to pray, break the chain of our prayers, the chain of graces will be broken, too; and as it is by this that we have to obtain salvation, we shall not be saved.

It is true that we cannot merit final perseverance, as the Council of Trent teaches: "It cannot be had from any other source but from him who is able to confirm the man who is standing that he may stand with perseverance."[120] Nevertheless, says St. Augustine, this great gift of perseverance can in a manner be merited by our prayers—that is, can be obtained by praying: "This gift, therefore, can be suppliantly merited; that is, can be obtained by supplication."[121] And F. Suarez adds that the man who prays infallibly obtains it. But to obtain it and to save ourselves, says St. Thomas, a persevering and continual prayer is necessary: "After baptism, continual prayer is necessary to a man in order that he may enter heaven."[122] And before this, our Savior himself had said it over and over again: "We ought always to pray, and not to faint" (Luke 18:1). Watch, therefore, praying at all times that you may be accounted worthy to escape all these things that are to come, and to stand before the Son of man" (Luke 21:36). The same had been previously said in the Old Testament, "Let nothing hinder you from praying always" (Sirach 18:22).

120. Sess. 6, c. 13.
121. *De Dono pers.*, c. 6.
122. *Summa*, p. 3, q. 39, a. 5.

"Bless God at all times, and desire him to direct your ways" (Job 4:20). Hence the Apostle inculcated on his disciples never to neglect prayer: "Pray without intermission" (1 Thessalonians 5:17). "Be instant in prayer, watching in it with thanksgiving" (Colossians 4:2). "I will therefore that men pray in every place" (1 Timothy 2:8). God does indeed wish to give us perseverance, says St. Nilus, but he will only give it to him who prays for it perseveringly: "He wills to confer benefits on him who perseveres in prayer."[123] Many sinners by the help of God's grace come to be converted and to receive pardon. But then because they neglect to ask for perseverance, they fall again and lose all.

Nor is it enough, says Bellarmine, to ask the grace of perseverance once or a few times; we ought always to ask it, every day till our death, if we wish to obtain it: "It must be asked day by day that it may be obtained day by day." He who asks it one day, obtains it for that one day; but if he does not ask it the next day, the next day he will fall.

And this is the lesson which our Lord wished to teach us in the parable of the man who would not give his loaves to his friend who asked him for them until he had become importunate in his demand: "Although he will not rise and give because he is his friend, yet because of his importunity, he will rise and give him as many as he needs (Luke 11:8). Now if this man, solely to deliver himself from the troublesome importunity of his friend, gave him even against his own will the loaves for which he asked, "How much more," says St. Augustine, "will the good God give, who both commands us to ask and is angry if we do not ask!"[124] How much more will God, who, as he is infinite goodness, has a commensurate desire to communicate to us his good things, how much more will he give his graces when we ask him for them! And the more as he himself tells us to ask for them, and as he is displeased when we do not demand them. God, then, does indeed wish to give us eternal life, and therein all graces; but he wishes also that we should never omit to ask him for them, even to the extent of being troublesome. Cornelius à Lapide says on the text just quoted, "God wishes us to be persevering in prayer to the extent of importunity."[125] Men of the world cannot bear the importunate; but God

123. *De Orat.*, c. 32.
124. Serm. 61, E. B.
125. *In Luc. xi. 8.*

not only bears with them, but wishes us to be importunate in praying to him for graces, and especially for perseverance. St. Gregory says that God wishes us to do him violence by our prayers; for such violence does not annoy but pleases him: "God wills to be called upon, he wills to be forced, he wills to be conquered by importunity. . . . Happy violence, by which God is not offended, but appeased !"[126]

So that to obtain perseverance we must always recommend ourselves to God, morning and night, at meditation, at Mass, at Communion, and always—especially in time of temptation, when we must keep repeating, "Lord, help me; Lord, assist me; keep your hand upon me; leave me not; have pity upon me!" Is there anything easier than to say, "Lord, help me, assist me!" The Psalmist says, "With me is prayer to the God of my life" (Psalm 42:9). On which the gloss is as follows: "A man may say, I cannot fast, I cannot give alms; but if he is told to pray, he can not say this, because there is nothing easier than to pray. But we must never cease praying; we must (so to speak) continually do violence to God that he may assist us always—a violence which is delightful and dear to him." "This violence is grateful to God," says Tertullian;[127] and St. Jerome says that the more persevering and importunate our prayers are, so much the more are they acceptable to God: "Prayer, as long as it is importunate, is more acceptable."[128]

"Blessed is the man who hears me, and who watches daily at my gates" (Proverbs 8:34). Happy is that man, says God, who listens to me and watches continually with holy prayers at the gates of my mercy. And Isaiah says, "Blessed are all they that wait for him" (Isaiah 30:18). Blessed are they who till the end wait (in prayer) for their salvation from God. Therefore in the Gospel Jesus Christ exhorts us to pray. But how? "Ask, and you shall receive; seek, and you shall find; knock, and it shall be opened to you" (Luke 11:9). Would it not have been enough to have said, "ask"? Why add, "seek," and "knock?" No, it was not superfluous to add them; for thereby our Savior wished us to understand that we ought to do as the poor who go begging. If they do not receive the alms they ask (I speak of licensed beggars), they do not cease asking; they return

126. *In Ps. paenit. vi.*
127. *Apolog.*, c. 39.
128. *Hom. in Matt.*

Part I

to ask again; and if the master of the house does not show himself any more, they set to work to knock at the door till they become very importunate and troublesome. That is what God wishes us to do: to pray, and to pray again, and never leave off praying that he would assist us and succor us, that he would enlighten us and strengthen us and never allow us to forfeit his grace. The learned Lessius[129] says that the man cannot be excused from mortal sin who does not pray when he is in sin or in danger of death; or, again, if he neglects to pray for any notable time, as (he says) for one or two months. But this does not include the time of temptations, because whoever finds himself assailed by any grievous temptation without doubt sins mortally if he does not have recourse to God in prayer, to ask for assistance to resist it—seeing that otherwise he places himself in a proximate, nay, in a certain, occasion of sin.

WHY GOD DELAYS GRANTING US FINAL PERSEVERANCE—
CONCLUSION

But, someone will say, since God can give and wishes to give me the grace of perseverance, why does he not give it me all at once, when I ask him?

The holy Fathers assign many reasons:

1. God does not grant it at once but delays it, first that he may better prove our confidence.

2. And further, says St. Augustine, that we may long for it more vehemently. Great gifts, he says, should be greatly desired; for good things soon obtained are not held in the same estimation as those which have been long looked for: "God wills not to give quickly that you may learn to have great desire for great things; things long desired are pleasanter to obtain, but things soon given are cheapened."[130]

3. Again, the Lord does so that we may not forget him; if we were already secure of persevering and of being saved, and if we had not continual need of God's help to preserve us in his grace and to save us, we should soon forget God. Want makes the poor keep resorting to the houses of the rich; so God, to draw us to himself, as St. Chrysostom

---

129. *De Just. et Jure*, book 2, c. 37. d. 3.
130. Serm. 61, E. B.

66

says, and to see us often at his feet, in order that he may thus be able to do us greater good, delays giving us the complete grace of salvation till the hour of our death: "It is not because he rejects our prayers that he delays, but by this contrivance he wishes to make us careful and to draw us to himself."[131] Again, he does so in order that we, by persevering in prayer, may unite ourselves closer to him with the sweet bonds of love: "Prayer," says the same St. Chrysostom, "which is accustomed to converse with God, is no slight bond of love to him."[132] This continual recurrence to God in prayer, and this confident expectation of the graces which we desire from him—oh, what a great spur and chain is it of love to inflame us and to bind us more closely to God!

But till what time have we to pray? Always, says the same saint, till we receive favorable sentence of eternal life—that is to say, till our death: "Do not leave off till you receive."[133] And he goes on to say that the man who resolves, "I will never leave off praying till I am saved," will most certainly be saved: "If you say, 'I will not give in till I have received,' you will assuredly receive." The Apostle writes that many run for the prize, but that he only receives it who runs till he wins: "Do you not know that they who run in the race, all run indeed, but one receives the prize? So run, that you may obtain" (1 Corinthians 9:24). It is not, then, enough for salvation simply to pray; but we must pray always that we may come to receive the crown which God promises, but promises only to those who are constant in prayer till the end.

So that if we wish to be saved, we must do as David did, who always kept his eyes turned to God, to implore his aid against being overcome by his enemies: "My eyes are ever toward the Lord, for he shall pluck my feet out of the snare" (Psalm 25:15). As the devil does not cease continually spreading snares to swallow us up, as St. Peter writes: "Your adversary, the devil, as a roaring lion, goes about, seeking whom he may devour" (1 Peter 5:8), so ought we ever to stand with our arms in our hands to defend ourselves from such a foe and to say, with the royal prophet, "I will pursue after my enemies; and I will not turn again till they are consumed" (Psalm 18:38). I will never cease fighting till I see my enemies

131. *In Gen.*, hom. 30.
132. *In Ps. iv.*
133. *In Matt.*, hom. 24.

conquered. But how can we obtain this victory, so important for us, and so difficult? "By most persevering prayers," says St. Augustine—only by prayers, and those most persevering. And till when? As long as the fight shall last. "As the battle is never over," says St. Bonaventure, "so let us never give over asking for mercy."[134] As we must be always in the combat, so should we be always asking God for aid not to be overcome. "Woe," says the wise man, "to him who in this battle leaves off praying: Woe to them that have lost patience" (Sirach 2:13–14). We may be saved, the Apostle tells us, but on this condition: if we retain a firm confidence and the glory of hope until the end" (Hebrews 3:6); if we are constant in praying with confidence until death.

Let us, then, take courage from the mercy of God and his promises, and say with the same Apostle, "Who then shall separate us from the love of Christ? Shall tribulation, or distress, or danger, or persecution, or the sword?" (Romans 8:35, 37). Who shall succeed in estranging us from the love of Jesus Christ? Tribulation, perhaps, or the danger of losing the goods of this world? The persecutions of devils or men? The torments inflicted by tyrants? "In all these we overcome"—it is St. Paul who encourages us—"because of him who has loved us." No, he says, no tribulation, no misery, danger, persecution, or torture shall ever be able to separate us from the love of Jesus Christ, because with God's help we shall overcome all if we fight for love of him who gave his life for us.

F. Hippolitus Durazzo, the day when he resolved to relinquish his dignity of prelate at Rome and to give himself entirely to God by entering the Society of Jesus (which he afterward did), was so afraid of being faithless by reason of his weakness that he said to God, "Do not forsake me, Lord, now that I have given myself wholly to you; for pity's sake, do not forsake me!" But he heard the whisper of God in his heart, "Do not you forsake me; rather," said God, "do I say to you, 'Do not forsake me.'" And so at last the servant of God, trusting in his goodness and help, concluded, "Then, O my God, you will not leave me, and I will not leave you."

Finally, if we wish not to be forsaken by God, we ought never to forsake praying to him not to leave us. If we do thus, he will certainly always assist us, and will never allow us to perish and to be separated

---

134. *De uno Conf.*, s. 5.

from his love. And to this end let us not only take care always to ask for final perseverance and the graces necessary to obtain it, but let us, at the same time, always by anticipation ask God for grace to go on praying; for this is precisely that great gift which he promised to his elect by the mouth of the prophet: "And I will pour out upon the house of David, and upon the inhabitants of Jerusalem, the spirit of grace and prayers" (Zechariah 12:10). Oh, what a great grace is the spirit of prayer—that is, the grace which God confers on a soul to enable it to pray always! Let us, then, never neglect to beg God to give us this grace and this spirit of continual prayer, because if we pray always, we shall certainly obtain from God perseverance and every other gift which we desire, since his promise of hearing whoever prays to him cannot fail. "For we are saved by hope" (Romans 8:24). With this hope of always praying, we may reckon ourselves saved. "Confidence will give us a broad entrance into this city."[135] This hope, said Venerable Bede, will give us a safe passage into the city of Paradise.

---

135. *In solemn. omn. SS.*, hom. 2.

Part II

Which Proves that the Grace of Prayer is Given to All, and Which Treats of the Ordinary Mode in Which This Grace Operates

Introduction

Taking, then, for granted that prayer is necessary for the attainment of eternal life, as we have proved in part I, chapter I, we should consequently also take for granted that everyone has sufficient aid from God to enable him actually to pray, without need of any further special grace; and that by prayer he may obtain all other graces necessary to enable him to persevere in keeping the commandments, and so gain eternal life; so that no one who is lost can ever excuse himself by saying that it was through want of the aid necessary for his salvation. For as God, in the natural order, has ordained that man should be born naked and in want of several things necessary for life, but then has given him hands and intelligence to clothe himself and provide for his other needs; so, in the supernatural order, man is born unable to obtain salvation by his own strength; but God in his goodness grants to everyone the grace of prayer, by which he is able to obtain all other graces which he needs in order to keep the commandments and to be saved.

But before I explain this point, I must prove two preliminary propositions: first that God wills all men to be saved, and therefore that Jesus Christ has died for all; secondly that God, on his part, gives to all men the graces necessary for salvation; whereby everyone may be saved if he corresponds to them.

CHAPTER I

God Wishes All Men to Be Saved, and therefore Christ Died to Save All Men

I.   God wishes all men to be saved

God loves all things that he has created: "For you love all things that are, and hate none of the things that you have made" (Wisdom 11:24). Now love cannot be idle: "All love has a force of its own, and cannot be idle," says St. Augustine.[136] Hence love necessarily implies benevolence, so that the person who loves cannot help doing good to the person beloved whenever there is an opportunity: "Love persuades a man to do those things which he believes to be good for him whom he loves," says Aristotle.[137] If, then, God loves all men, he must in consequence will that all should obtain eternal salvation, which is the one and sovereign good of man, seeing that it is the one end for which he was created: "You have your fruit unto sanctification; but your end, eternal life" (Romans 6:22).

This doctrine that God wishes all men to be saved, and that Jesus Christ died for the salvation of all, is now a certain doctrine taught by the Catholic Church, as theologians in common teach, namely, Petavius, Gonet, Gotti, and others, besides Tourneley, who adds that it is a doctrine all but of faith.

1. DECISION OF THE CHURCH

With reason, therefore, were the predestinarians condemned who, among their errors, taught (as may be seen in Noris, Petavius, and more

---

136.   *In Ps. cxxi.*
137.   *Rhetor.*, book 2, c. 4.

especially in Tourneley) that God does not will all men to be saved; as Hincmar, Archbishop of Rheims, testifies of them in his first letter, where he says, "The ancient predestinarians asserted that God does not will all men to be saved, but only those who are saved." These persons were condemned, first in the Council of Arles, A.D. 475, which pronounced, "anathema to him that said that Christ did not die for all men, and that he does not will all to be saved."[138] They were next condemned in the Council of Lyons, A.D. 490, where Lucidus was forced to retract and confess, "I condemn the man who says that Christ did not suffer death for the salvation of all men." So also in the ninth century, Gotheschalcus, who renewed the same error, was condemned by the Council of Quercy, A.D. 853, in the third article of which it was decided, "God wills all men, without exception, to be saved, although all men be not saved"; and in the fourth article: "There is no man for whom Christ did not suffer, although all men are not redeemed by the mystery of his Passion." The same error was finally condemned in the twelfth and thirteenth Propositions of Quesnel. In the former it was said, "When God wills to save a soul, the will of God is undoubtedly effectual"; in the latter, "All whom God wills to save through Christ are infallibly saved." These propositions were justly condemned precisely because they meant that God does not will all men to be saved; since from the proposition that those whom God wills to be saved are infallibly saved, it logically follows that God does not will even all the faithful to be saved, let alone all men.

This was also clearly expressed by the Council of Trent, in which it was said that Jesus Christ died, "that all might receive the adoption of sons," and in chapter three, "But though he died for all, yet all do not receive the benefits of his death."[139] The Council then takes for granted that the Redeemer died not only for the elect, but also for those who, through their own fault, do not receive the benefit of Redemption. Nor is it of any use to affirm that the Council only meant to say that Jesus Christ has given to the world a ransom sufficient to save all men; for in this sense we might say that he died also for the devils. Moreover, the Council of Trent intended here to reprove the errors of those innovators who, not denying that the

---

138. *Anath.* 6.
139. Sess. 6., c. 2–3.

blood of Christ was sufficient to save all, yet asserted that in fact it was not shed and given for all; this is the error which the Council intended to condemn when it said that our Savior died for all. Further, in chapter six it says that sinners are put in a fit state to receive justification by hope in God through the merits of Jesus Christ: "They are raised to hope, trusting that God will be merciful to them through Christ."[140] Now, if Jesus Christ had not applied to all the merits of his Passion, then, since no one (without a special revelation) could be certain of being among the number of those to whom the Redeemer had willed to apply the fruit of his merits, no sinner could entertain such hope, not having the certain and secure foundation which is necessary for hope—namely, that God wills all men to be saved and will pardon all sinners prepared for it by the merits of Jesus Christ. And this, besides being the error formerly condemned in Baius, who said that Christ had only died for the elect, is also condemned in the fifth proposition of Jansen: "It is Semi-Pelagianism to say that Christ died or shed his blood for all men." And Innocent X, in his Constitution of A.D. 1653, expressly declared that to say Christ died for the salvation of the elect only is an impious and heretical proposition.

2. THE CELEBRATED TEXT OF ST. PAUL

On the other hand, both the Scriptures and all the Fathers assure us that God sincerely and really wishes the salvation of all men and the conversion of all sinners, as long as they are in this world. For this we have, first of all, the express text of St. Paul: "Who will have all men to be saved, and to come to the knowledge of the truth" (1 Timothy 2:4). The sentence of the Apostle is absolute and indicative God wills all men to be saved. These words in their natural sense declare that God truly wills all men to be saved; and it is a certain rule, received in common by all that the words in Scripture are not to be distorted to an unnatural sense, except in the sole case when the literal meaning is repugnant to faith or morals. St. Bonaventure writes precisely to our purpose when he says, "We must hold that when the Apostle says God wills all men to be saved, it is necessary to grant that he does will it."[141]

---

140. Sess. 6, c. 6.
141. *In 1 Sent.*, d. 46, a. 1, q. 1.

It is true that St. Augustine and St. Thomas mention different interpretations which have been given to this text, but both these Doctors understand it to mean a real will of God to save all, without exception.

And concerning St. Augustine, we shall see just now that this was his true opinion; so that St. Prosper protests against attributing to him the supposition that God did not sincerely wish the salvation of all men, and of each individual, as an aspersion on the holy Doctor. Hence the same St. Prosper, who was a most faithful disciple of his, says, "It is most sincerely to be believed and confessed that God wills all men to be saved, since the Apostle (whose very words these are) is particular in commanding that prayers should be made to God for all."[142]

The argument of the saint is clear, founded on St. Paul's words in the above-cited passage: "I beseech therefore, first of all that prayers should be made for all men," and then he adds, "For this is good and acceptable before God our Savior, who wills all men to be saved." So the Apostle wishes us to pray for all, exactly in the same sense that God wishes the salvation of all. St. Chrysostom uses the same argument: "If he wills all to be saved, surely we ought to pray for all. If he desires all to be saved, do you also be of one mind with him."[143] And if in some passages in his controversy with the Semi-Pelagians, St. Augustine seems to have held a different interpretation of this text, saying that God does not will the salvation of each individual, but only of some, Petavius well observes that here the holy Father speaks only incidentally, not with direct intention; or, at any rate that he speaks of the grace of that absolute and victorious will (*voluntas absoluta et victrix*) with which God absolutely wills the salvation of some persons, and of which the saint elsewhere says, "The will of the Almighty is always invincible."[144]

Let us hear how St. Thomas uses another method of reconciling the opinion of St. Augustine with that of St. John Damascene, who holds that antecedently God wills all and each individual to be saved: "God's first intention is to will all men to be saved that as good he may make us partakers of his goodness; but after we have sinned, he wills to punish

---

142. *Resp. ad 2 obj. Vincent.*
143. *In 1 Tim.*, hom. 7.
144. *Enchir.*, c. 102.

us as just."[145] On the other hand, St. Augustine (as we have seen) seems in a few passages to think differently. But St. Thomas reconciles these opinions and says that St. Damascene spoke of the antecedent will of God, by which he really wills all men to be saved, while St. Augustine spoke of the consequent will. He then goes on to explain the meaning of antecedent and consequent will: "Antecedent will is that by which God wills all to be saved; but when all the circumstances of this or that individual are considered, it is found to be good that all men should be saved; for it is good that he who prepares himself and consents to it should be saved; but not he who is unwilling and resists, etc. And this is called the consequent will because it presupposes a foreknowledge of a man's deeds, not as a cause of the act of will, but as a reason for the thing willed and determined."

So that St. Thomas was also of opinion that God truly wills all men and each individual to be saved. This opinion he reasserts in several other places. On the text, "Him that comes to me I will not cast out" (John 6:37), he quotes St. Chrysostom, who makes our Lord say, "If then I was incarnate for the salvation of men, how can I cast them out?" And this is what he means when he says, "Therefore I cast them not out, because I came down from heaven to do my Father's will, who wills all men to be saved."[146] And again, "God, by his most liberal will, gives [grace] to everyone that prepares himself"—who wills all men to be saved—"and therefore the grace of God is wanting to no man, but as far as he is concerned, he communicates it to everyone."[147] Again, he declares the same thing more expressly in his explanation of the text of St. Paul, "God wills all men to be saved." "In God," he says, "the salvation of all men, considered in itself, belongs to that class of things which he wishes, and this is his antecedent will; but when the good of justice is taken into consideration, and the rightness of punishing sin, in this sense he does not will the salvation of all, and this is his consequent will."[148] Here we may see how consistent St. Thomas was in his explanation of antecedent and consequent will; for he here repeats what he had said in the passage quoted a

---

145. *De Fid. Orth.*, book 2, c. 29.
146. *In Joan. vi.*, lect. 4.
147. *In Heb. xii.*, lect. 3.
148. *In 1 Tim. 2*, lect. 1.

little before. In this place he only adds the comparison of a merchant who antecedently wills to save all his merchandise; but if a tempest comes on, he willingly throws it overboard in order to preserve his own life. In like manner, he says, God, considering the iniquity of some persons, wills them to be punished in satisfaction of his justice and consequently does not will them to be saved; but antecedently, and considered in itself, he wills with a true desire the salvation of all men. So that, as he says in the former passage, God's will to save all men is on his part absolute; it is only conditional on the part of the object willed—that is, if man will correspond to what the right order demands in order to be saved. "Nor yet," he says, "is there imperfection on the part of God's will, but on the part of the thing willed; because it is not accepted with all the circumstances which are required, in order to be saved in the proper manner."[149] And he again and more distinctly declares what he means by antecedent and consequent will: "A judge antecedently wishes every man to live, but he consequently wishes a murderer to be hanged; so God antecedently wills every man to be saved, but he consequently wills some to be damned; in consequence, that is, of the exigencies of his justice."[150]

I have no intention here of blaming the opinion that men are predestined to glory previously to the prevision of their merits; I only say that I cannot understand how those who think that God, without any regard to their merits, has elected some to eternal life and excluded others can therefore persuade themselves that he wills all to be saved—unless, indeed, they mean that this will of God is not true and sincere, but rather a hypothetical or metaphorical will. I cannot understand, I say, how it can be maintained that God wills all men to be saved and to partake of his glory when the greater part of them have been already excluded from this glory antecedently to any demerit on their part. Petavius says, in defense of his contrary opinion, what was the use of God's giving to all men the desire of eternal happiness, when he had excluded the majority of them from it antecedently to any demerits of theirs? What was the use of Jesus Christ's coming to save all men by his death, when so many poor creatures had been already deprived by God of all benefit

---

149.   *In 1 Sent.*, d. 46, q. 1, a. 1.
150.   *Summa*, p. 1, q. 19, a. 6.

therefrom? What was the use of giving them so many means of salvation, when they had been already excluded from the attainment of the end? Therefore, adds Petavius (and this is a most weighty reflection), if this ever was the case, we must say that God, who loves all things that he has created, yet in creating mankind did not love them all but rather utterly detested the greater part of them, in excluding them from the glory for which he had created them. It is certain that the happiness of a creature consists in the attainment of the end for which it was created. On the other hand, it is certain that God creates all men for eternal life. If, therefore, God, having created some men for eternal life, had thereupon, without regard to their sins, excluded them from it, he would in creating them have utterly hated them without cause and would have done them the greatest injury they could possibly suffer in excluding them from the attainment of their end—that is, of the glory for which they had been created "For," says Petavius in a passage which we abridge, "God cannot feel indifferent between love and hatred toward his creatures, especially toward men, whom he either loves to eternal life or hates to damnation; but it is the greatest evil of man to be alienated from God and to be reprobate; wherefore, if God wills the everlasting destruction of any man's soul, he does not love him but hates him with the greatest hatred possible, in that kind which transcends the natural order." And by this eternal ruin, or "everlasting destruction," he does not mean the positive damnation which God destines for certain individuals, but simply the exclusion from glory; since in fact, as Tertullian says, of what use would it ever be to us that God had not created us for hell if in creating us he had separated us from the number of his elect, since the separation from the elect necessarily implies the loss of salvation and therefore damnation; since there is no mean between them. "For what," says Tertullian, "will be the end of the separated? Will it not be the loss of salvation?"[151] Whence Petavius concludes, "Wherefore, if God loves every man with a love which is antecedent to their merits, he does not hate his soul, and therefore he does not desire the greatest evil to him."[152] If, therefore, God loves all men, as is certain, we ought to hold that he wills all to be saved,

151. *Adv. Marc.*, book 4.
152. *De Deo.*, book 10, c. 3, n. 5.

and that he has never hated anyone to such a degree that he has willed to do him the greatest evils by excluding him from glory previously to the prevision of his demerits.

I say notwithstanding, and repeat again and again that I cannot understand it; for this matter of predestination is so profound a mystery that it made the Apostle exclaim: "Oh, the depth of the riches of the wisdom and the knowledge of God! How incomprehensible are his judgments, and how unsearchable his ways! For who has known the mind of the Lord?" (Romans 11:44). We ought to submit ourselves to the will of God, who has chosen to leave this mystery in obscurity to his Church, that we all might humble ourselves under the deep judgments of his divine Providence. And the more because divine grace, by which alone men can gain eternal life, is dispensed more or less abundantly by God entirely gratuitously and without any regard to our merits. So that to save ourselves it will always be necessary for us to throw ourselves into the arms of the divine mercy, in order that he may assist us with his grace to obtain salvation, trusting always in his infallible promises to hear and save the man who prays to him.

3. OTHER TEXTS OF SCRIPTURE

But let us return to our point that God sincerely wills all men to be saved. There are other texts which prove the same thing, as when God says: "As I live, says the Lord, I do not desire the death of the wicked, but that the wicked man turns from his way and lives" (Ezekiel 33:11). He not only says that he wills not the death, but that he wills the life of a sinner; and he swears, as Tertullian observes, in order that he may be more readily believed in this: "When moreover he swears, saying, "As I live," he desires to be believed."[153]

Further, David says, "For wrath is in his indignation, and life in his will" (Psalm 30:6). If he chastises us, he does it because our sins provoke him to indignation; but as to his will, he does not will our death but our life: "Life in his will." St. Basil says about this text that God wills all to be made partakers of life. David says elsewhere, "Our God is the God of salvation; and of the Lord are the issues from death" (Psalm 68:21).

---

153. *De Paenit.*

On this Bellarmine says, "This is proper to him, this is his nature; our God is a saving God, and his are the issues from death—that is, liberation from it," so that it is God's proper nature to save all and to deliver all from eternal death.

Again, our Lord says, "Come to me, all you that labor and are burdened, and I will refresh you" (Matthew 11:28). If he calls all to salvation, then he truly wills all to be saved. Again, St. Peter says: "He does not will that any should perish, but that all should return to penance" (2 Peter 3:9). He does not will the damnation of anyone, but he wills that all should do penance and so should be saved.

Again, our Lord says: "I stand at the gate and knock; if anyone will open, I will enter" (Revelation 3:30). "Why will you die, O house of Israel? Return and live" (Ezekiel 18:31). "What is there that I ought to do more to my vineyard that I have not done to it?" (Isaiah 5:4) "How often would I have gathered together your children, as the hen gathers her chickens under her wings, and you would not!" (Matthew 23:37). How could our Lord have said that he stands knocking at the heart of us sinners? How exhort us so strongly to return to his arms? How reproach us by asking what more he could have done for our salvation? How say that he has willed to receive us as children, if he had not a true will to save all men? Again, St. Luke relates that our Lord, looking over Jerusalem from a distance and contemplating the destruction of its people because of their sin, "seeing the city, he wept over it" (Luke 19:41). Why did he weep, then, says Theophylact (after St. Chrysostom), seeing the ruin of the Jews, unless it was because he really desired their salvation? Now then, after so many attestations of our Lord in which he makes known to us that he wills to see all men saved, how can it ever be said that God does not will the salvation of all? "But if these texts of Scripture," says Petavius, "in which God has testified his will in such clear and often-repeated expressions, nay, even with tears and with an oath, may be abused and distorted to the very opposite sense, namely, that God determined to send all mankind (except a few) to perdition, and never had a will to save them, what dogma of faith is so clear as to be safe from similar injury and cavil ?"[154] This great writer says that to deny that God really wills the salvation of

---

154. *De Deo.*, book 10, c. 15, n. 5.

all men is an insult and cavil against the plainest doctrines of the faith. And Cardinal Sfondrati adds, "Those who think otherwise seem to me to make God a mere stage-god—like those people who pretend to be kings in a play, when indeed they are anything but kings."[155]

4. GENERAL CONSENT OF THE FATHERS

Moreover, this truth that God wills all men to be saved is confirmed by the general consent of the Fathers. There can be no doubt that all the Greek Fathers have been uniform in saying that God wills all and each individual to be saved. So St. Justin, St. Basil, St. Gregory, St. Cyril, St. Methodius, and St. Chrysostom, all adduced by Petavius. But let us see what the Latin Fathers say.

St. Jerome: "[God] wills to save all; but since no man is saved without his own will, he wills us to will what is good that when we have willed, he may also will to fulfill his designs in us";[156] and in another place, "God therefore willed to save those who desire (to be saved); and he invited them to salvation that their will might have its reward; but they would not believe in him."[157]

St. Hilary: "God would that all men were saved, and not those alone who are to belong to the number of the elect, but all absolutely, so as to make no exception."[158]

St. Paulinus: "Christ says to all, 'Come to me,' etc.; for he, the Creator of all men, so far as he is concerned, wills every man to be saved."[159]

St. Ambrose: "Even with respect to the wicked he had to manifest his will [to save them], and therefore he could not pass over his betrayer that all might see that in the election even of the traitor he exhibits [his desire] of saving all . . . and, so far as God is concerned, he shows to all that he was willing to deliver all."[160]

The author of the work known as the *Commentaries of St. Ambrose* (supposed by Petavius to be Hilary the Deacon), in speaking of the text

155. *Nodus praed.*, p. 1, s. 1.
156. *In Eph.* 1.
157. *In Is. lxiii.*
158. *Ep. ad Aug.*
159. *Ep. 24. ad Sever.*
160. *De Parad.*, c. 8.

of St. Paul ("Who wills all men," etc.), asks this question: "But since God wills that all should be saved, as he is Almighty, why are there so many who are not saved?" And he answers: "He wills them to be saved, if they also are willing; for he who gave the law excluded no one from salvation. . . . This medicine is of no use to the unwilling." He says that God has excluded no one from glory, and that he gives grace to all to be saved, but on condition that they are willing to correspond to it, because his grace is of no use to the man who rejects it. St. Chrysostom in like manner asks, "Why then are not all men saved, if God wills all to be saved?" and he answers, "Because every man's will does not coincide with his will, and he forces no man."[161] St. Augustine: "God wills all men to be saved, but not so as to destroy their free will."[162] He says the same thing in several other places, which we shall shortly have to produce.

II. Jesus Christ died to save all men

That Jesus Christ, therefore, died for all and each of mankind, is clear not only from the Scriptures, but from the writings of the Fathers. Great, certainly, was the ruin which the sin of Adam occasioned to the whole human race; but Jesus Christ, by the grace of Redemption, repaired all the evils which Adam introduced. Hence the Council of Trent has declared that baptism renders the soul pure and immaculate, and that the sin which remains in it is not for its harm, but to enable it to gain a higher crown if it resists so as not to consent to it: "For in the regenerate God hates nothing . . . they are made innocent, immaculate, pure, and beloved of God. . . . But this holy synod confesses and feels that concupiscence, or the fuel [of sin], remains in baptized persons; but as it was left for our probation, it cannot injure those who do not consent to it; nay, rather, he who contends lawfully [against it] shall be crowned."[163] Thus, as St. Leo says, "We have gained greater things by the grace of Christ than we had lost through the envy of the devil."[164] The gain which we have made by the redemption of Jesus Christ is greater than the loss which we suffered

---

161. *De Mut. Nom.*, hom. 3, E. B.
162. *De Spir. et Litt.*, c. 33.
163. Sess. 5, *De pecc. or.*, n. 5.
164. *De Asc.*, s.1.

by the sin of Adam. The Apostle plainly declared this when he said, "Not as the offense, so also the gift. For where the offense abounded, there did grace more abound" (Romans 5:15, 20). Our Lord says the same: "I am come that they may have life, and have it more abundantly" (John 10:10). David and Isaiah had predicted it: "With him is plentiful redemption" (Psalm 130:7). "She has received of the hand of the Lord double for all her sins" (Isaiah 40:2). About which words the interpreter says, "God has so forgiven iniquities through Christ that men have received double—that is, very much greater good—instead of the punishment of sin which they deserved."

Now that our Savior, as I said, died for all, and that he offered the work of his redemption to the Eternal Father for the salvation of each one, the holy Scriptures assure us of the following:

1. THE TESTIMONY OF HOLY SCRIPTURE

"The Son of Man came to save that which was lost" (Matthew 18:11). "Who gave himself a redemption for all" (1 Timothy 2:6). "Christ died for all, that they also who live may not now live to themselves, but to him who died for them" (2 Corinthians 5:15). "For hereunto we labor and are reviled, because we hope in the living God, who is the Savior of all men, especially of the faithful" (1 Timothy 4:10). "And he is the propitiation for our sins; and not for ours only, but also for those of the whole world" (1 John 2:2). "For the love of Christ presses us, judging this, that if one died for all, then all were dead" (2 Corinthians 5:14). And to speak only of this last text, I ask, how could the Apostle ever have concluded that all were dead because Christ died for all, unless he had been certain that Christ had really died for all? And the more, because St. Paul uses this truth as an argument for the love which it should kindle in us toward our Savior. But by far the best passage to exhibit the desire and wish which God has to save all men is another text of St. Paul: "He that spared not his own Son, but delivered him for us all" (Romans 8:32). The force of this passage is increased by what follows: "How has he not also with him given us all things?" If God has given us all things, how can we henceforth fear that he has denied us the election to glory, always on condition that we correspond (to his grace)? And if he has given us his Son, says Cardinal Sfondrati, how will he deny us the grace to be saved? "Here he clearly instructs us [he is speaking of St. Paul], that God assures us that he will not refuse us the less after he has given the greater; that he will not deny us grace to save ourselves after giving his Son that we might be saved."[165] And in truth, how could St. Paul have said that God, in giving us his Son, has given us all things if the Apostle had believed that God had excluded many from the glory which is the one good and the one end for which they were created? Has then God given "all things" to these "many" and yet denied them the best thing, namely, eternal happiness, without which (as there is no middle way) they cannot but be eternally miserable? Unless we would say another thing still more unseemly, as another learned author well observes, namely, that God gives to all the grace to attain glory but then refuses to allow many to enter on its enjoyment—that he gives the means and refuses the end.

For the rest, all the holy Fathers agree in saying that Jesus Christ died to obtain eternal salvation for all men.

St. Jerome: "Christ died for all; he was the only one who could be offered for all because all were dead in sins."[166]

St. Ambrose: "Christ came to cure our wounds; but since all do not search for the remedy . . . therefore he cures those who are willing; he does not force the unwilling."[167] In another place: "He has provided for all men the means of cure, so that whoever perishes may lay the blame of his death on himself because he would not be cured when he had a remedy; and that, on the other hand, the mercy of Christ to all may be openly proclaimed, who wills that all men should be saved."[168] And more clearly still in another place: "Jesus did not write his will for the benefit of one, or of few, but of all; we are all inscribed therein as his heirs; the legacy is in common and belongs by right to all; the universal heritage, belonging wholly to each."[169] Mark the words, "We are all inscribed as heirs; the Redeemer has written us all down as heirs of heaven."

---

165. *Nod. Praed.*, p. 1, s. 2, n. 1.
166. *In 2 Cor. v.*
167. *In Ps. lxxii.*
168. *De Abel.*, book 2, c. 3.
169. *In Ps. cxviii*, s. 14.

St. Leo: "As Christ found no one free from guilt, so he came to deliver all."[170]

St. Augustine, on the words of St. John, "For God did not send his Son to judge the world, but that the world might be saved through him" (John 3:17), says: "So, as far as it lies with the physician, he came to heal the sick man."[171] Mark the words "as far as it lies with the physician." For God, as far as he is concerned, effectually wills the salvation of all, but (as St. Augustine goes on to say) cannot heal the man who will not be healed: "He heals universally, but he heals not the unwilling."[172] "For what can be happier for you than, as you have your life in your hands, so to have your health depend on your will?" When he says, "he heals," he speaks of sinners who are sick and unable to get well by their own strength; when he says "universally" (*omnino*), he declares that nothing is wanting on God's part for sinners to be healed and saved. Then when he says, "As you have your life in your hands, so your health depends on your will," he shows that God for his part really wills us all to be saved; otherwise, it would not be in our power to obtain health and eternal life. In another place, "He who redeemed us at such a cost does not will that we perish; for he does not purchase in order to destroy, but he redeems in order to give life."[173] He has redeemed us all, in order to save us all. And hence he encourages all to hope for eternal bliss in that celebrated sentence: "Let human frailty raise itself; let it not say, 'I shall never be happy.' . . . It is a greater thing that Christ has done than that which he has promised. What has he done? He has died for you. What has he promised? That you shall live with him."[174]

Some have pretended to say that Jesus Christ offered his blood for all in order to obtain grace for them but not salvation. But Petrocorensis will not hear of this opinion, of which he says: "O disputatious frivolity! How could the wisdom of God will the means of salvation without willing its end?"[175] St. Augustine, moreover, speaking against the Jews, says: "You

---

170.   *In Nat. Dom.*, s. 1.
171.   *In Jo. tr.* 12.
172.   *In Ps. cii.*
173.   Serm. 22, E. B.
174.   *In Ps. cxlviii.*
175.   Book 3, c. 3, q. 4.

acknowledge the side which you pierced, that it was opened both by you and for you."[176] If Jesus Christ had not really given his blood for all, the Jews might have answered St. Augustine, that it was quite true they had opened the side of our Savior, but not that it was opened for them.

In like manner, St. Thomas has no doubt that Jesus Christ died for all; whence he deduces that he wills all to be saved: "Christ Jesus is mediator between God and men; not between God and some men, but between him and all men; and this would not be unless he willed all to be saved."[177] This is confirmed, as we have already said, by the condemnation of the fifth proposition of Jansen, who said, "It is semi-Pelagianism to assert that Christ died or shed his blood for all men." The sense of this, according to the context of the other condemned propositions and according to the principles of Jansen, is as follows: Jesus Christ did not die to merit for all men the graces sufficient for salvation, but only for the predestined; or, in Jansen's own expressed words, "It is in no way consonant to the principles of Augustine to think that Christ our Lord died or shed his blood for the eternal salvation either of unbelievers, who die in their unbelief, or of the just who do not persevere."[178] Therefore the contrary and Catholic belief is as follows: It is not semi-Pelagianism, but it is right to say that Jesus Christ died to merit not only for the predestinate but for all, even for the reprobate, grace sufficient to obtain eternal salvation in the ordinary course of Providence.

Further, that God truly, on his part, wills all men to be saved, and that Jesus Christ died for the salvation of all, is certified to us by the fact that God imposes on us all the precept of hope. The reason is clear. St. Paul calls Christian hope the anchor of the soul, secure and firm: "Who have fled for refuge to hold fast the hope set before us which we have as an anchor of the soul, sure and firm" (Hebrews 6:18). Now in what could we fix this sure and firm anchor of our hope except in the truth that God wills all to be saved? "With what confidence," says Petrocorensis, "will men be able to hope for God's mercy if it is not certain that God wills the salvation of all of them? With what confidence will they offer the death of Christ to God, in order to obtain pardon, if it is uncertain whether

176. *De Symb. ad cat.*, book 2, c. 8.
177. *In 1 Tim. 2*, lect. 1.
178. *De Grat. Chr.*, c. 20.

he was offered up for them?"[179] And Cardinal Sfondrati says that if God had elected some to eternal life and excluded others, we should have a greater motive to despair than to hope; seeing that, in fact, the elect are much fewer than the damned: "No one could have a firm hope, since he would have more grounds of despair than of hope; for the reprobate are much more numerous than the elect."[180] And if Jesus Christ had not died for the salvation of all, how could we have a sure ground to hope for salvation through the merits of Jesus Christ, without a special revelation? But St. Augustine had no doubt when he said, "All my hope, and the certainty of my faith, is in the precious blood of Christ, which was shed for us and for our salvation."[181] Thus the saint placed all his hope in the blood of Jesus Christ because the faith assured him that Christ died for all. But we shall have a better opportunity of examining this question of hope in chapter III, where we shall establish the principal point, namely, that the grace of prayer is given to all.

III. Children who die without baptism

Here it only remains for us to answer the objection which is drawn from children being lost when they die before baptism and before they come to the use of reason. If God wills all to be saved, it is objected, how is it that these children perish without any fault of their own, since God gives them no assistance to attain eternal salvation? There are two answers to this objection, the latter more correct than the former. I will state them briefly.

First, it is answered that God, by antecedent will, wishes all to be saved and therefore has granted universal means for the salvation of all; but these means at times fail of their effect, either by reason of the unwillingness of some persons to avail themselves of them, or because others are unable to make use of them on account of secondary causes (such as the death of children), whose course God is not bound to change after having disposed the whole according to the just judgment of his general Providence; all this is collected from what St. Thomas says. Jesus

179. Book 3, c. 3, q. 4.
180. *Nod. praed.*, p. 1, s. 1.
181. *Medit.*, c. 14.

Christ offered his merits for all men and instituted baptism for all; but the application of this means of salvation, so far as relates to children who die before the use of reason, is not prevented by the direct will of God but by a merely permissive will, because as he is the general provider of all things, he is not bound to disturb the general order to provide for the particular order.

The second answer is that to perish is not the same as not to be blessed, since eternal happiness is a gift entirely gratuitous; and therefore the want of it is not a punishment. The opinion, therefore, of St. Thomas is very just that children who die in infancy have neither the pain of sense nor the pain of loss; not the pain of sense, he says, "because pain of sense corresponds to conversion to creatures; and in original sin there is not conversion to creatures" (as the fault is not our own), "and therefore pain of sense is not due to original sin," because original sin does not imply an act.[182] Objectors oppose to this the teaching of St. Augustine, who in some places shows that his opinion was that children are condemned even to the pain of sense. But in another place he declares that he was very much confused about this point. These are his words: "When I come to the punishment of infants, I find myself (believe me) in great straits; nor can I at all find anything to say."[183] And in another place he writes that it may be said that such children receive neither reward nor punishment: "Nor need we fear that it is impossible there should be a middle sentence between reward and punishment; since their life was midway between sin and good works."[184] This was directly affirmed by St. Gregory Nazianzen: "Children will be sentenced by the just judge neither to the glory of heaven nor to punishment."[185] St. Gregory of Nyssa was of the same opinion: "The premature death of children shows that they who have thus ceased to live will not be in pain and unhappiness."[186]

And as far as relates to the pain of loss, although these children are excluded from glory, nevertheless St. Thomas,[187] who had reflected most

---

182. *De Mal.*, q. 5, a. 2.
183. Epist. 166, E. B.
184. *De Lib. Arb.*, book 3, c. 23.
185. *Serm. in S. Lav.*
186. *De Infant. etc.*
187. *In 2 Sent.*, d. 33, q. 2, a. 2.

deeply on this point, teaches that no one feels pain for the want of that good of which he is not capable; so that as no man grieves that he cannot fly, or no private person that he is not emperor, so these children feel no pain at being deprived of the glory of which they were never capable, since they could never pretend to it either by the principles of nature, or by their own merits. St. Thomas adds, in another place,[188] a further reason, which is that the supernatural knowledge of glory comes only by means of actual faith, which transcends all natural knowledge; so that children can never feel pain for the privation of that glory, of which they never had a supernatural knowledge. He further says, in the former passage, that such children will not only not grieve for the loss of eternal happiness, but will, moreover, have pleasure in their natural gifts and will even in some way enjoy God, so far as is implied in natural knowledge and in natural love: "Rather will they rejoice in this: that they will participate much in the divine goodness and in natural perfections." And he immediately adds that, although they will be separated from God as regards the union of glory, nevertheless, "They will be united with him by participation of natural gifts and so will even be able to rejoice in him with a natural knowledge and love."[189]

---

188. *De Mal.*, q. 5, a. 3.
189. *In 2 Sent.*, d. 33, q. 2, a. 2.

God Commonly Gives to All the Just the Grace Necessary for the Observance of the Commandments, and to All Sinners the Grace Necessary for Conversion

I. Proofs

If, then, God wills all to be saved, it follows that he gives to all that grace and those aids which are necessary for the attainment of salvation, otherwise it could never be said that he has a true will to save all. "The effect of the antecedent will," says St. Thomas, "by which God wills the salvation of all men is that order of nature the purpose of which is our salvation, and likewise those things which conduce to that end and which are offered to all in common, whether by nature or by grace."[190] It is certain—in contradiction to the blasphemies of Luther and Calvin that God does not impose a law that is impossible to be observed. On the other hand, it is certain that without the assistance of grace, the observance of the law is impossible; as Innocent I declared against the Pelagians when he said, "It is certain that as we overcome by the aid of God, so without his aid we must be overcome."[191] Pope Celestine declared the same thing. Therefore, if God gives to all men a possible law, it follows that he also gives to all men the grace necessary to observe it, whether immediately or mediately by means of prayer, as the Council of Trent has most clearly defined: "God does not command impossibilities; but by commanding

---

190. *In 1 Sent.*, d. 46, q. 1, a. 1.
191. *Rescr. ad Conc. Carthag.*

he admonishes you both to do what you can and to ask for that which is beyond your power, and by his help enables you to do it."[192] Otherwise, if God refused us both the proximate and remote grace to enable us to fulfill the law, either the law would have been given in vain, or sin would be necessary, and if necessary would be no longer sin, as we shall shortly prove at some length.

1. TEACHING OF THE FATHERS OF THE GREEK CHURCH

And this is the general opinion of the Greek Fathers:

St. Cyril of Alexandria says: "But if a man endowed as others, and equally with them, with the gifts of divine grace has fallen by his own free will, how shall Christ be said not to have saved even him, since he delivered the man, since he gave him the necessary aid to avoid sin."[193] How, says the saint, can that sinner who has received the assistance of grace equally with those who remained faithful, and has of his own accord chosen to sin, how can he blame Jesus Christ, who has, as far as he is concerned, delivered him by means of the assistance granted to him? St. John Chrysostom asks: "How is it that some are vessels of wrath, others vessels of mercy?" And he answers, "Because of each person's free will; for, since God is very good, he manifests equal kindness to all." Then, speaking of Pharaoh, whose heart is said in Scripture to have been hardened, he adds, "If Pharaoh was not saved, it must all be attributed to his will, since no less was given to him than to those who were saved."[194] And in another place, speaking of the petition of the mother of Zebedee's sons, on the words, "It is not mine to give , etc." (Matthew 20:23), he observes: "By this Christ wished to show that it was not simply his to give, but that it also belonged to the combatants to take; for if it depended only on himself, all men would be saved."[195]

St. Isidore of Pelusium: "For God wills seriously, and in all ways, to assist those who are wallowing in vice, so that he may deprive them of all excuse."[196]

---

192. Sess. 6, c. 2.
193. *In Jo.*, book 2, c. 21.
194. *In Rom.*, hom. 16.
195. *Hom. in loco cit. cont. Anom.*
196. Book 2, c. 270.

St. Cyril of Jerusalem: "God has opened the gate of eternal life so that, as far as he is concerned, all may gain it without anything to hinder them."[197]

But the doctrine of these Greek Fathers does not suit Jansen, who has the temerity to say that they have spoken most imperfectly on grace: "None have spoken in grace more imperfectly than the Greeks." In matters of grace, then, are we not to follow the teaching of the Greek Fathers, who were the first masters and columns of the Church? Perhaps the doctrine of the Greeks, especially in this important matter, was different from that of the Latin Church? On the contrary, it is certain that the true doctrine of faith came from the Greek to the Latin Church; so that, as St. Augustine wrote against Julian, who opposed to him the authority of the Greek Fathers, there can be no doubt that the faith of the Latins is the same as that of the Greeks. Whom, then, are we to follow? Shall we follow Jansen, whose errors have already been condemned as heretical by the Church—who had the audacity to say that even the just have not the grace requisite to enable them to keep certain precepts, and that man merits and demerits, even though he acts through necessity, provided he is not forced by violence; these and all his other errors springing from his most false system of the delectation relatively victorious, of which we shall speak at length when we confute him in chapter III.

2. TEACHING OF THE FATHERS OF THE LATIN CHURCH

But since the Greek Fathers do not satisfy Jansen, let us see what the Latins say on this subject. But they in no wise differ from the Greeks.

St. Jerome says, "Man can do no good work without God, who, in giving free will, did not refuse his grace to aid every single work."[198] Mark the words "did not refuse his grace for every single work." St. Ambrose: "He would never come and knock at the door unless he wished to enter; it is our fault that he does not always enter."[199] St. Leo: "Justly does he insist on the command, since he furnishes beforehand aid to keep it."[200] St. Hilary: "Now the grace of justification has abounded through one gift

---

197. *Catech.* 18.
198. *Ep. ad Cyprian. presb.*
199. *In Ps. cxviii.*, s. 12.
200. *De Pass.*, s. 16.

to all men."[201] Innocent I: "He gives to man daily remedies; and unless we put confidence in them and depend upon them, we shall never be able to overcome human errors."[202]

St. Augustine: "It is not imputed to you as a sin if you are ignorant against your will, but if you neglect to learn that of which you are ignorant. Nor is it imputed as a sin that you do not bind up your wounded limbs, but [mark this] that you despise him who is willing to cure you. These are your own sins; for no man is deprived of the knowledge of how to seek with benefit to himself." In another place: "Therefore if the soul is ignorant what it is to do, it proceeds from this that it has not yet learned; but it will receive this knowledge if it has made a good use of what it has already received; for it has received in this that it can piously and diligently seek, if it will"—mark the words—"it has received power to seek piously and diligently."[203] So that everyone receives at least the remote grace to seek; and if he makes good use of this, he will receive the proximate grace to perform that which at first he could not do. St. Augustine founds all this on the principle that no man sins in doing that which he cannot help; therefore, if a man sins in anything, he sins in that he might have avoided it by the grace of God, which is wanting to no man: "Who sins in that which cannot in any way be helped? But a man does sin, therefore it might have been helped."[204] "But only by his aid, who cannot be deceived."[205] An evident reason, by which it becomes quite clear (as we shall have to show further on, when we speak of the sin of the obstinate) that if the grace necessary to observe the commandments were wanting, there would be no sin.

St. Thomas teaches the same in several places. In one place, in explaining the text, "Who wills all men to be saved" (1 Timothy 2:4), he says, "And therefore grace is wanting to no man, but [as far as God is concerned] is communicated to all; as the sun is present even to the blind."[206] So that as the sun sheds its light upon all, and only those are deprived of it who

---

201. *In Ps. lix.*
202. *Rescr. ad Conc. Carthag.*
203. *De Lib. Arb.*, book 3, c. 19, 22.
204. *De Lib. Arb.*, book 3, c. 18.
205. *De Nat. et Gr.*, c. 67.
206. *In Heb. 12*, lect. 3.

voluntarily blind themselves to its rays, so God communicates to all men grace to observe the law; and men are lost simply because they will not avail themselves of it. In another place: "It belongs to divine Providence to provide all men with what is necessary to salvation, if only there be no impediment on man's part."[207] If, then, God gives all men the graces necessary for salvation, and if actual grace is necessary to overcome temptations and to observe the commandments, we must necessarily conclude that he gives all men either immediately or mediately actual grace to do good; and when mediately, no further grace is necessary to enable them to put in practice the means (such as prayer) of obtaining actual proximate grace. In another place, on the words of St. John's Gospel, "No man comes to me," etc., he says, "If the heart of man is not lifted up, it is from no defect on the part of him who draws it, who as far as he is concerned never fails; but from an impediment caused by him who is being drawn."[208]

Scotus says the same: "God wills to save all men, so far as rests with him, and with his antecedent will, by which he has given them the ordinary gifts necessary to salvation."[209] The Council of Cologne in 1536: "Although no one is converted except he is drawn by the Father, yet let no one pretend to excuse himself on the plea of not being drawn. He stands at the gate and knocks, by the internal and the external Word."[210]

3. TESTIMONY OF HOLY SCRIPTURE

Nor did the Fathers speak without warrant of the Holy Scriptures; for God in several places most clearly assures us that he does not neglect to assist us with his grace if we are willing to avail ourselves of it, either for perseverance if we are in a state of justification, or for conversion if we are in sin.

"I stand at the gate and knock; if any man shall hear my voice and open to me the gate, I will come in to him" (Revelation 3:20). Bellarmine reasons well on this text that our Lord, who knows that man cannot open without his grace, would knock in vain at the door of his heart unless he

---

207. *De Ver.*, q. 14, a. 11.
208. *In Jo. 6*, lect. 5.
209. *In 1 Sent.*, d. 46, q. un.
210. P. 7, c. 32.

had first conferred on him the grace to open when he will. This is exactly what St. Thomas teaches in explaining the text; he says that God gives everyone the grace necessary for salvation, so that he may correspond to it if he will: "God by his most liberal will gives grace to everyone who prepares himself: 'Behold I stand at the door and knock.'"[211] "And therefore the grace of God is wanting to no one, but communicates itself to all men, as far as it is concerned." In another place, he says, "It is the business of God's Providence to provide everyone with what is necessary to salvation." So that, as St. Ambrose says, the Lord knocks at the gate because he truly wishes to enter; if he does not enter, or if after entering he does not remain in our souls, it is because we prevent him from entering, or drive him out when he has entered: "Because he comes and knocks at the door, he always wishes to enter; but it is through us that he does not always go in, nor always remain."[212]

"What is there that I ought to do more to my vineyard that I have not done to it? Was it that I expected that it should bring forth grapes, and it has brought forth wild grapes?" (Isaiah 50:4). Bellarmine says on these words, "If he had not given the power to bring forth grapes, how could God say, 'I expected'?" And if God had not given to all men the grace necessary for salvation, he could not have said to the Jews, "What is there that I ought to have done more?" For they could have answered that if they had not yielded fruit, it was for lack of necessary assistance. Bellarmine says the same on the words of our Lord, "How often would I have gathered together your children, and you would not?" (Matthew 23:37). "How did he wish to be sought for by the unwilling unless he helps them, so that they may be able to be willing?"

"We have received your mercy, O God, in the midst of your temple" (Psalm 48:10). On this St. Bernard observes: "Mercy is in the midst of the temple—not in any hole and corner—because there is no acceptance of persons with God."[213] It is placed in public, it is offered to all, and no one is without it except he who refuses it."

"Or do you despise the riches of His goodness? Do you not know not that the benignity of God leads you to penance?"(Romans 2:4). You

211. *In Heb. 12*, lect. 3.
212. *In Ps. cxviii.*, s. 12.
213. *In Purif. B. V.*, s. 1.

95

see that it is through his own malice that the sinner is not converted, because he despises the riches of the divine goodness which calls him and never ceases to move him to conversion by his grace. God hates sin but, at the same time, never ceases to love the sinful soul while it remains on earth and always gives it the assistance it requires for salvation: "But you spare all because they are yours, O Lord, who loves souls" (Wisdom 11:27). Hence we see, says Bellarmine, that God does not refuse grace to resist temptations to any sinner, however obstinate and blinded he may be: "Assistance to avoid new sin is always at hand for all men, either immediately or mediately [i.e., by means of prayer], so that they may ask further aid from God, by the help of which they will avoid sin."[214] Here we may quote what God says by Ezekiel: "As I live, says the Lord God, I do not desire the death of the wicked, but that the wicked turn from his way and live" (Ezekiel 33:11). St. Peter says the same: "He bears patiently for your sakes, not willing that any should perish, but that all should return to penance" (2 Peter 3:9). If, therefore, God wishes that all should actually be converted, it must necessarily be held that he gives to all the grace which they need for actual conversion.

II. Obstinate or hardened sinners, and the abandonment of them by God

I know well that there are theologians who maintain that God refuses to certain obstinate sinners even sufficient grace. And, among others, they avail themselves of a position of St. Thomas, who says: "But although they who are in sin cannot through their own power avoid putting or interposing an obstacle to grace—unless they are prevented by grace, as we have shown—nevertheless, this also is imputed to them as a sin because this defect is left in them from previous sin, as a drunken man is not excused from murder committed in that drunkenness which was incurred by his own fault. Besides, although he who is in sin has not this in his own power, that he altogether avoid sin, yet he has power at this present moment to avoid this or that sin, as has been said; so that whatever he commits, he commits voluntarily; and therefore it is properly

---

214. *De Gr. et Lib. Arb.*, book 2, c. 7.

imputed to him as sin."[215] From this they gather that St. Thomas intends to say that sinners can indeed avoid particular sins but not all sins, because in punishment for sins previously committed they are deprived of all actual grace.

But we answer that here St. Thomas is not speaking of actual but of habitual or sanctifying grace, without which the sinner cannot keep himself long from falling into new sins, as he teaches in several places. And that he means the same in the passage just quoted is clear from the context, which we must here transcribe, in order to understand the true meaning of the saint.

In the first place, the title of chapter 160, where the quotation occurs, is as follows: "That man, when he is in sin, cannot avoid sin without grace." The very title shows that St. Thomas intended no more than he has said in the other places which we have referred to.

Moreover, in the course of the chapter, he says: "For when the mind of man has declined from the state of uprightness, it is manifest that it has fallen from its relation, "order" [*ordo*], to its true end. . . . Whensoever, therefore, anything shall have occurred to the mind conducive to the inordinate end, but improper for the true end, it will be chosen, unless the mind is brought back to its due relation, so as to prefer its true end to all others; and this is the effect of grace. But while anything repugnant to our last end is the object of our choice, it puts a hindrance in the way of the grace which conducts us to that end; whence it is manifest that, after sinning, man cannot altogether abstain from sin before he is brought back by grace to the due order. And hence the opinion of the Pelagians is shown to be absurd, that man, being in sin, can without grace avoid [fresh] sin." And then he goes on with the sentence quoted above: "But although they," etc., of which our opponents make use.

So that, in the first place, the intention of St. Thomas is not to prove that some sinners are deprived of all actual grace and therefore, being unable to avoid all sin, they do commit sin and are worthy of punishment; but his intention is to prove against the Pelagians that a man who remains without sanctifying grace cannot abstain from sinning. And we see that he is here certainly speaking of sanctifying grace, for this is that which

---

215. *Contra Gent.*, book 3, c. 160.

alone brings the soul back to the right order. It is of this same sanctifying grace that he intends to speak when he says immediately after, "Except he is prevented by the assistance of grace"—by which he means that if the sinner is not prevented, that is, is not previously informed (*informato*) by grace and brought back to the right order of holding God to be his last end, he cannot avoid committing fresh sins. And this is the meaning of the Thomists, for instance, of Ferrariensis (Silvestre) and Father Gonet in their comments on this passage. But without having recourse to other authors, it is quite clear from what St. Thomas himself says in his *Summa*, where he discusses the same point and brings forward the identical reasons in the same words as in the 160th chapter of his book *Contra Gentes*; and there he expressly says that he is only speaking of habitual or sanctifying grace.

And it is impossible that the holy Doctor could have meant otherwise, since he elsewhere teaches that, on the one hand, God's grace is never wanting to anyone, as he says in his commentary on St. John: "But lest you might suppose that this effect was consequent on the removal of the true light, the Evangelist, to obviate this opposition, adds that was the true light which enlightens every man. For the Word enlightens, so far as he is concerned, because on his part he is wanting to no one but wishes all men to be saved. But if anyone is not enlightened, this is the fault of the man who turns himself away from the light that would enlighten him."[216] And, on the other hand, he teaches that there is no sinner so lost and abandoned by grace as not to be able to lay aside his obstinacy and to unite himself to the will of God, which he certainly cannot do without the assistance of grace: "During this life there is no man who cannot lay aside obstinacy of mind and so conform to the divine will."[217] In another place he says, "So long as the use of free will remains to a man in this life . . . he can prepare himself for grace by being sorry for his sins." But no one can make an act of sorrow for sin without grace. In another place he says, "No man in this life can be so obstinate in evil but that it is possible for him to cooperate to his own deliverance."[218] "To cooperate" necessarily implies grace to cooperate with.

216. *In Jo. 1*, lect. 5.
217. *In 1 Sent.*, d. 48, q. 1, a. 3.
218. *In 4 Sent.*, d. 20, q. 1, a. 1.

In another place he observes, on the text of St. Paul, "He wills all to be saved," "Therefore the grace of God is wanting to no man; but, as far as it is concerned, it communicates itself to all." Again, on the same words, "God, so far as he is concerned, is prepared to give grace to all men. . . . Those, therefore, only are deprived of grace who permit a hindrance to grace to exist in themselves; and, therefore, they cannot be excused if they sin."[219] And when St. Thomas says, "God is prepared to give grace to all," he does not mean actual grace, but only sanctifying grace.

Cardinal Gotti justly contradicts those who say that God keeps ready at hand the aids necessary for salvation but, in matter of fact, does not give them to all. Of what use would it be to a sick man (says this learned author) if the physician only kept the remedies ready and then would not apply them? Then he concludes (quite to the point of our argument) that we must necessarily say, "God not only offers but also confers on every individual, even on infidels and hardened sinners, help sufficient to observe the commandments, whether it be proximate or remote."[220]

For the rest, St. Thomas says that it is only the sins of the devils and the damned that cannot be wiped out by penance; but, on the other hand, "to say that there is any sin in this life of which a man cannot repent is erroneous . . . because this doctrine would derogate from the power of grace."[221] If grace were wanting to anyone, certainly he could not repent. Moreover, as we have already seen, St. Thomas expressly teaches in several places, and especially in his comment on Hebrews 12, that God, as far as he is concerned, refuses to no man the grace necessary for conversion: "The grace of God is wanting to no man; but, as far as it is concerned, communicates itself to all." So that the learned author of the *Theology* for the use of the seminary of Peterkau says, "It is a calumny to impute to St. Thomas that he taught that any sinners were totally deserted by God."[222]

Bellarmine makes a sound distinction on this point and says that, for avoiding fresh sins, every sinner has at all times sufficient assistance, at least mediately: "The necessary and sufficient assistance for the avoidance of sin is given by God's goodness to all men at all times, either

---

219. *Contra Gent.*, book 3, c. 159.
220. *De Div. Vol.*, q. 2, d. 3, s. 2.
221. *Summa*, p. 3, q. 86, a. 1.
222. Book 3, c. 3, q. 4.

immediately or mediately. . . . We say 'or mediately' because it is certain that some men have not that help by which they can immediately avoid sin, but yet have the help which enables them to obtain from God greater safeguards, by the assistance of which they will avoid sins."[223] But for the grace of conversion, he says that this is not given at all times to the sinner; but that no one will be ever so far left to himself "as to be surely and absolutely deprived of God's help through all this life, so as to have cause to despair of salvation."[224]

And so say the theologians who follow St. Thomas. Thus Soto: "I am absolutely certain, and I believe that all the holy Doctors who are worthy of the name were always most positive, that no one was ever deserted by God in this mortal life."[225] And the reason is evident; for if the sinner was quite abandoned by grace, either his sins afterward committed could no longer be imputed to him, or he would be under an obligation to do that which he had no power to fulfill; but it is a positive rule of St. Augustine that there is never a sin in that which cannot be avoided: "No one sins in that which can by no means be avoided."[226] And this is agreeable to the teaching of the Apostle: "But God is faithful, who will not suffer you to be tempted above that which you are able; but will also make with the temptation issue that you may be able to bear it" (1 Corinthians 10:13). The word "issue" means the divine assistance which God always gives to the tempted to enable them to resist, as St. Cyprian explains it: "He will make with the temptation a way of escape."[227] And Primasius more clearly: "He will so order the issue that we shall be able to endure; that is, in temptation he will strengthen you with the help of his grace, so that you may be able to bear it." St. Augustine and St. Thomas go so far as to say that God would be unjust and cruel if he obliged anyone to a command which he could not keep. St. Augustine says, "It is the deepest injustice to reckon any one guilty of sin for not doing that which he could not do."[228] And St. Thomas: "God is not more cruel than man;

---

223. *De Gr. et Lib. Arb.*, book 2, c. 7.
224. *Ibid.*, c. 6.
225. *De Nat. et Gr.*, book 1, c. 18.
226. *De Lib. Arb.*, book 3, c. 18.
227. *Testim.*, book 3, n. 91.
228. *De Duab. An.*, c. 12.

but it is reckoned cruelty in a man to oblige a person by law to do that which he cannot fulfill; therefore we must by no means imagine this of God."[229] "It is, however, different," he says, "when it is through his own neglect that he has not the grace to be able to keep the commandments,"[230] which properly means, when man neglects to avail himself of the remote grace of prayer, in order to obtain the proximate grace to enable him to keep the law, as the Council of Trent teaches: "God does not command impossibilities but by commanding admonishes you to do what you can and to ask for that which is beyond your power; and by his help enables you to do it."[231]

St. Augustine repeats his decision in many other places, that there is no sin in what cannot be avoided. In one he says, "Whether there is iniquity or whether there is justice, if it was not in the man's power, there can be no just reward, no just punishment."[232] Elsewhere he says, "Finally, if no power is given them to abstain from their works, we cannot hold that they sin."[233] Again: "The devil, indeed, suggests; but with the help of God it is in our power to choose or to refuse his suggestions. And so, when by God's help it is in your power, why do you not rather determine to obey God than him?"[234] Again, "No one, therefore, is answerable for what he has not received."[235] Again, "No one is worthy of blame for not doing that which he cannot do."[236]

Other Fathers have taught the same doctrine. So St. Jerome, "We are not forced by necessity to be either virtuous or vicious; for where there is necessity, there is neither condemnation nor crown."[237] Tertullian: "For a law would not be given to him who had it not in his power to observe it duly."[238] Marcus the Hermit: "Hidden grace assists us, but it depends

---

229. *In 2 Sent.*, d. 28, q. 1, a. 3.
230. *De Ver.*, q. 24, a. 14.
231. Sess. 6, c. 11.
232. *Cont. Faust.*, book 22, c. 78.
233. *De Duab. An.*, c. 12.
234. Serm. 253, E. B. app.
235. *De Lib. Arb.*, book 3, c. 16.
236. *De Duab. An.*, c. 11.
237. *Cont. Jov.*, book 2.
238. *Cont. Marcion*, book 2.

on us to do or not to do good according to our strength."[239] So also St. Irenaeus, St. Cyril of Alexandria, St. Chrysostom, and others.

Nor is there any difficulty in what St. Thomas says, that grace is denied to some persons in punishment of original sin: "To whomsoever the assistance of grace is given, it is given through simple mercy; but from those to whom it is not given, it is withheld justly in punishment of previous sin, or at least of original sin, as Augustine says."[240] For, as Cardinal Gotti well observes, St. Augustine and St. Thomas are speaking of actual proximate grace to satisfy the precepts of faith and charity, of which, indeed, St. Thomas is speaking in this place; but, for all this, they do not intend to deny that God gives every man interior grace, by means of which he may at any rate obtain by prayer the grace of faith and of salvation; since, as we have already seen, these holy Doctors do not doubt that God grants to every man at least remote grace to satisfy the precepts. Here we may add the authority of St. Prosper, who says, "All men enjoy some measure of heavenly teaching; and though the measure of grace is small, it is sufficient to be a remedy for some and to be a testimony for all."[241]

Nor could it be understood otherwise; for if it were true that any had sinned for want of even remote sufficient grace, withheld through original sin being imputed to them as a fault, it would follow that the liberty of will, which by a figure of speech we are said to have had in the sin of Adam, would be sufficient to make us actual sinners. But this cannot be said, as it is expressly condemned in the first proposition of Michael Baius, who said, "That liberty which caused sin to be voluntary and free in its cause, namely, in original sin and in the liberty of Adam when sinning is sufficient to [cause] formal sin [in us], and to make us deserve punishment." Against this proposition we may make use of what Bellarmine said,[242] that to commit a personal sin distinct from the sin of Adam a new exertion of free will is requisite, and a free will distinct from that of Adam, otherwise there is no distinct sin; according to the doctrine of St. Thomas, who teaches, "For a personal sin, absolute personal

---

239. *De Just. ex op.*, c. 56.
240. *Summa*, 2.2, q. 2, a. 5. August., *De Corr. et Grat.*, c. 11.
241. *De Voc. Gent.*, book 2, c. 15.
242. *De Gr. et Lib. Arb.*, book 2, c. 7.

liberty is requisite." Further, with respect to the baptized, the Council of Trent has declared that in them there remains nothing to condemn: "God hates nothing in the regenerate; for there is no condemnation to them who are truly buried with Christ by baptism unto death." And it is added that concupiscence is not left in us as a punishment, "but for our trial; and it cannot harm those who do not consent to it."[243] On the contrary, the concupiscence left in us would do exceedingly great harm to man if, on account of it, God denied him even the remote grace necessary to obtain salvation.

From all this, several theologians conclude that to say that God refuses to anyone sufficient help to enable him to keep the commandments would be contrary to the faith, because in that case God would oblige us to impossibilities. So says F. Nunez: "God never refused aid sufficient to keep the commandments, otherwise they could not be in any way fulfilled; and thus we should have the heresy of Luther back again, that God has obliged men to impossibilities."[244] And in another place, "It is of faith, so that the opposite doctrine is a manifest heresy, that every man, while he is alive, can do penance for his sins."[245] And Father Ledesma, "It is a certain truth of faith that that is not sin which is not in the free power of man."[246]

Giovenino says that the sinner becomes guilty through the exercise of free will in choosing voluntarily this or that sin—though at the time he is necessitated to sin because he is without actual grace sufficient to deliver him from all sin. But this doctrine, that a man when fallen sins, not having liberty to do otherwise than to choose what sin he will commit and necessitated to commit some sin, justly offends Monseigneur de Saléon, Archbishop of Vienna, who, in his book *Jansenismus Redivivus*, writes as follows: "Who will endure to hear that a man once fallen, being deprived of grace, can enjoy no other liberty than that of choosing one sin rather than another, being necessitated to sin in some way."[247] So that a criminal condemned to death, who has no other liberty allowed him than

---

243. Sess. 5, *De Pecc. or.*, n. 5.
244. *In* 1.2, *q.* 109, *a.* 8.
245. *In* p. 3, *q.* 86, *a.* 1, *d.* 1.
246. *De Aux.*, q. un., a. 18.
247. P. 2, a. 6.

to choose whether he will die by the sword, by poison, or by fire, may be said, when he has made his choice, to die a voluntary and free death. And how can sin be imputed to a man who must sin in some way or another? The 67th of the condemned Propositions of Baius is as follows: "Man sins damnably even in that which he does through necessity." How can there be liberty where there is necessity to sin? Jansen answers that the liberty of will, which by a figure of speech we are said to have had in Adam's sin, is sufficient to make us sinners. But this, too, was condemned in Baius' first proposition, "That liberty," etc., as we have seen above.

Our opponents go on to say that though the sinner abandoned by grace cannot avoid all mortal sins collectively, yet he can avoid each sin distributively or individually, "by a simple suspension or negation of activity," as they say. But this cannot be admitted for several reasons. First, because when a vehement temptation is assailing us, which it requires much strength to resist, it cannot morally be overcome (as all theologians agree) except by the assistance of grace or else by yielding to another, but opposite, vicious passion; so that a sinner deprived of grace would be irremediably necessitated to sin in one or the other way—which it is horrible to affirm, as we have already shown. Secondly, when we are urged by a great concupiscence to sin in a particular way, there is not always—nay, it seldom happens that there is—another improper motive urging us to the contrary course, of sufficient force to hinder us from committing the first sin; so that, when this second motive is absent or weak, then it would be necessary for the sinner to commit that particular sin to which he feels inclined. Thirdly, this abstaining from sin "by a simple negation of activity," as they say, can hardly be imagined in sins against the negative precepts but, as Tourneley and Gotti well observe, is altogether impossible in cases where a positive precept obliges us to do some supernatural act—as, for instance, to make an act of faith, hope, love, and contrition. For as these acts are supernatural, they necessarily require the supernatural assistance of God to enable us to perform them. So that, at any rate in this case, if grace were wanting, man would be necessitated to sin by not satisfying the positive precept, although he was unable to avoid the sin. But to assert this is, as F. Bannez observes, contrary to faith: "A man cannot sin without having first actually received an inspiration of divine grace. We assert this conclusion to be certainly of faith; because no one sins in not doing that which he cannot do, as it is certain *de fide*; but a man to whom nothing more is given than the bare faculties of human nature has no power to act above nature, and therefore does not sin in omitting to perform a supernatural act."[248]

Nor will it do to say that if the sinner is deprived of grace, he is deprived of it by his own fault; and therefore, though he is deprived of grace, yet he sins. For Cardinal Gotti well replies to this that God can justly punish the sinner for his previous faults, but not for his future transgressions of precepts which he is no longer able to fulfill. If a servant, he says, were sent to a place, and if he, through his own fault, fell into a pit, his master might punish him for his carelessness in falling and even for his subsequent disobedience, if means (such as a rope or ladder) were given him to get out of the pit, and he would not avail himself of them; but supposing that his master did not help him to get out, he would be a tyrant if he ordered him to proceed and punished him for not proceeding. Hence he concludes, "When, therefore, a man has by sin fallen into the ditch and become unable to proceed on his way to eternal life, though God may punish him for this fault, and also if he refuses the offer of grace to enable him to proceed; yet if God chose to leave him to his own weakness, he cannot without injustice oblige him to proceed on the way, nor punish him if he does not proceed."[249]

Moreover, our opponents adduce many texts of Scripture where this abandonment is apparently expressed: "Blind the heart of this people . . . lest they see with their eyes . . . and be converted, and I heal them" (Isaiah 6:10). "We would have cured Babylon, but she is not healed; let us forsake her" (Jeremiah 51:9). "Add iniquity upon their iniquity, and let them not come into your justice" (Psalm 69:28). "For this cause God delivered them up to shameful affections. He has mercy on whom he will; and whom he will he hardens" (Romans 1:26, 9:18), and others similar. But it is usually and easily answered to all these in general that in the Holy Scriptures God is often said to do what he only permits; so that if we would not blaspheme with Calvin and say that God positively

248. *In* p. 1, q. 23, a. 3, concl. 3.
249. *De Div. Vol.*, q. 2, d. 3, s. 3.

destines and determines some persons to sin, we must say that God permits some sinners, in penalty of their faults, to be on the one hand assailed by vehement temptations (which is the evil from which we pray God to deliver us when we say, "Lead us not into temptation") and, on the other hand, that they remain morally abandoned in their sin; so that their conversion, and the resistance they should make to temptation, although neither impossible nor desperate, is yet, through their faults and their bad habits, very difficult; since, in their laxity of life, they have only very rare and weak desires and motions to resist their bad habits and to regain the way of salvation. And this is the imperfect obstinacy of the hardened sinner which St. Thomas describes: "He is hardened who cannot easily cooperate in his escape from sin; and this is imperfect obstinacy, because a man may be obstinate in this life if he has a will so fixed upon sin that no motions toward good arise, except very weak ones."[250] On one side, the mind is obscured and the will is hardened against God's inspirations and attached to the pleasures of sense, so as to despise and feel disgust for spiritual blessings; the sensual passions and appetites reign in the soul through the bad habits that have been acquired; on the other side, the illuminations and the callings of God are, by its own fault, rendered scarcely efficacious to move the soul, which has so despised them and made so bad a use of them that it even feels a certain aversion toward them, because it does not want to be disturbed in its sensual gratifications. All these things constitute moral abandonment; and when a sinner has once fallen into it, it is only with the utmost difficulty that he can escape from his miserable state and bring himself to live a well-regulated life.

In order to escape and pass at once from such disorder to a state of salvation, a great and extraordinary grace would be requisite; but God seldom confers such a grace on these obstinate sinners. Sometimes he gives it, says St. Thomas, and chooses them for vessels of mercy, as the Apostle calls them, in order to make known his goodness; but to the rest he justly refuses it and leaves them in their unhappy state in order to show forth his justice and power: "Sometimes," says the Angel of the Schools, "out of the abundance of his goodness he prevents with his assistance

---

250. *De Ver.*, q. 24, a. 11.

even those who put a hindrance in the way of his grace, and converts them, etc. And as he does not enlighten all the blind nor cure all the sick, so neither does he assist all who place an impediment to his grace, so as to convert them. . . . This is what the Apostle means when he says that God, 'to show forth his anger and to make his power known, endured with much patience the vessels of wrath, fitted for destruction, that he might show the riches of his glory upon the vessels of mercy, which he has prepared unto glory'" (Romans 9:22–23). Then he adds, "But since out of the number of those who are involved in the same sins there are some to whom God gives the grace of conversion, while others he only endures or allows to go on in the course of things, we are not to inquire the reason why he converts some and not others. For the Apostle says, 'Has not the potter power over the clay, to make of the same mass one vessel to honor, and another to dishonor?'" (Romans 9:21).[251] We do not then deny (to bring this point to a conclusion) that there is such a thing as the moral abandonment of some obstinate sinners, so that their conversion is morally impossible, that is to say, very difficult. And this concession is abundantly sufficient for the laudable object which our opponents have in defending their opinion, which is to restrain evil-doers and to induce them to consider before they come to fall into such a deplorable state. But then it is cruelty (as Petrocorensis well says) to take from them all hope and entirely to shut against them the way of salvation by the doctrine that they have fallen into so complete an abandonment as to be deprived of all actual grace to enable them to avoid fresh sins and to be converted; at any rate, mediately by means of prayer (which is not refused to any man while he lives, as we shall prove in the last chapter), whereby they can afterward obtain abundant help for placing themselves in a state of salvation: since the fear of total abandonment would not only lead them to despair, but also to give themselves more completely to their vices, in the belief that they are altogether destitute of grace, so that they have no hope left of escaping eternal damnation.

---

251. *Cont. Gent.*, book 3, c. 161.

Exposition and Confutation of Jansen's System of "Delectation Relatively Victorious"

I.   The System of Jansen

In the following chapter we will, as we promised, demonstrate that the grace of prayer is given to all men. But this doctrine does not please Jansen; he goes so far as to call it a hallucination: "It is a hallucination to think that the grace of prayer is always present to a man."[252] According to his system, he considers that without the delectation relatively victorious we cannot pray; but this delight is not granted to all men; therefore (he adds), all men have not sufficient grace and power to fulfill the commandments, for many are without even the remote grace to enable them to pray as they ought or indeed to pray at all. "Since, therefore," he continues, "most men either do not ask for grace to enable them to fulfill the law or do not ask for it as is necessary; and since God does not give all men the grace either to pray fervently, or even to pray at all; it is most evident that many of the faithful are without that sufficient grace and consequently without that perpetual power of fulfilling the one precept (of the moment) which some theologians proclaim." Before, then, we prove our own position, we must confute his pernicious system, from which all his errors are derived; and we must show that not we, but that he, is laboring under a hallucination.

All know the five propositions of Jansen which were condemned by

---

252.   *De Gr. Chr.*, book 3, c. 13.

the Church as heretical.[253] Now, as Tourneley proves, all these propositions follow if you once grant his system of preponderating delectation, on which Jansen founds all his doctrine.[254] F. Ignatius Graveson says the same: "From this pernicious principle Jansen and his followers derived these erroneous conclusions (the five propositions), which are most intimately connected and form one system with that principle."[255] So F. Berti, who says that "from the principle of the two invincible delectations, as from a root, almost all the other Jansenist errors have sprung, and especially the five condemned propositions."[256] And Father Fortunate da Brescia, in his lately published book called *A Confutation of the System of Cornelius Jansen*, proves to demonstration that, admitting this system, you must necessarily admit the five condemned propositions.

Let us, therefore, distinctly exhibit this system of Jansen. He says that the will of man, since the fall of Adam, is unable to do otherwise than to follow either the pleasure of grace (which he calls the celestial delectation) or that of concupiscence (which he calls earthly delectation), according as one prevails over the others. So that if the heavenly delectation is greater, then it necessarily overcomes the other; if the earthly delectation preponderates, then the will necessarily yields to it.

And here we must remark that Jansen does not hereby intend deliberate or consequent delectation, for thus he would be in accord with all Catholic Doctors; since, when the pleasure we take in a thing is deliberate, and embraced not from necessity but from free choice of the will, then certainly it is necessary that the will should act according to the

---

253.   For the benefit of the reader we here subjoin the five propositions: (1) Some commandments of God are impossible to just men who wish to fulfill them and who, for this purpose, make efforts according to the strength that they at present possess; and the grace that would render them possible is wanting to them. (2) In the state of fallen nature one never resists interior grace. (3) To merit or demerit in the state of fallen nature, there is not required in man freedom from interior necessity (*libertas a necessitate*). (4) The Semi-Pelagians admitted the necessity of an interior preventing grace for every act, even for the beginning of faith; they were heretics in that they maintained that the will of man can submit to this grace or resist it. (5) It is a Semi-Pelagian error to say that Jesus Christ died or shed his blood for all men without exception. These five propositions were condemned by Innocent X in 1653.—*Ed.*

254.   *De Gr. Chr.*, q. 3. *De Jans.*, ep. 3.

255.   *Ep. cl.* 1, *ep.* 1.

256.   *Aug. syst. Vind.*, d. 4, c. 1, s. 8.

delectation. But Jansen intends indeliberate delectation, and in this sense he understands the celebrated saying of St. Augustine: "It is necessary that our act should follow the greater pleasure."[257] Now, as we shall presently show, this sentence must necessarily be understood of deliberate and consequent delectation; but Jansen falsely interprets (and on this false interpretation founds his whole doctrine) that it means indeliberate delectation, antecedent to any act of the will. So that, in his system, there is no such thing as sufficient grace; since it is either of too little weight and necessarily insufficient, or else it preponderates over the concupiscence and is then necessarily efficacious, since he makes the whole efficacy of grace consist in the relative preponderance of the indeliberate delectation: "There will be no such thing as sufficient grace"—these are his words—"but it will be either efficient, or so inefficient that no act can follow from it."[258]

When this system is once laid down, all the five condemned propositions follow as necessary conclusions from it. Let us omit the others and speak here exclusively of the first and third as being most to our purpose.

REFUTATION OF THE FIRST PROPOSITION

The first is, "Some commands of God are impossible to just men, who wish to fulfill them and endeavor to do so, according to the strength they at present possess. Moreover, grace is wanting to them, whereby these precepts may become possible."[259] Some precepts (says he) become impossible even to the just, who have the will and strive to observe them, in proportion as they want the grace which should prevail over concupiscence: "Unless the heavenly delectation is greater than the earthly, it cannot but happen that we are overcome by the infirmity of our will." And again: "While carnal delectation is in vigor, it is impossible that the thought of virtue should prevail."[260] Although, said Jansen, grace regarded absolutely in itself, and apart from act and circumstance, may be abundantly sufficient to move the will to virtue, nevertheless, rela-

257. *In Gal.*, n. 49.
258. *De Gr. Chr.*, book 4, c. 10.
259. *Ibid.*, book 3, c. 13.
260. *Ibid.*, book 4, c. 6–9.

tively considered—that is, when the carnal delectation is greater than the heavenly (for when the carnal preponderates over grace, it is always accompanied by the act of will)—then grace is completely insufficient to draw to itself the consent of the will. And, as Father Graveson well observes, the absolute power to keep the commandments, which many would have by virtue of grace, whenever it is derived from a grace which is less than the concupiscence is actually no longer power but a true impotence, since the will is then entirely unable to act rightly, as the less weight cannot outweigh the greater.

How, then, can a man be blamed for not fulfilling the precept when he is without grace even sufficient to enable him to do so? The objection is strong and is most manifestly just; so much so that Jansen himself can not help putting it, "How is it that they are not excused who are without this assistance, since without it they would not be able to fulfill the precept?"[261] Let us see how he answers this question. The difficulty is great, therefore he attempts to disembarrass himself of it in several ways.

1. He answers that inability excuses when a man wishes to fulfill the precept but cannot, but not when he does not wish to fulfill it. But we answer that when the will, according to his principles, is necessarily obliged to yield to the indeliberate pleasure of the concupiscence because of its outweighing grace, it is then physically impossible for a man to wish to fulfill the precept; since, supposing the preponderance of the carnal pleasure, grace has no longer sufficient active strength to overcome it. And of this principle Jansen has no doubt, for he says that the stronger delectation intrinsically determines and insuperably moves the will to accept it, so that the will is then completely deprived of relative power to resist. "Whence it follows," says Father Graveson, "that this necessity, according to the doctrine of Jansen and his disciples, is not a moral but an antecedent and invincible necessity, which cannot be admitted without open heresy."[262] Jansen says, moreover, that except the delectation of grace preponderates, it is as impossible for a man to fulfill the precept as it is "for one without wings to fly, for the blind to see, for the deaf to hear, or for a man with broken limbs to walk straight."[263] It would be the

261. *De Gr. Chr.*, book 3, c. 15.
262. *Ep. cl.* 2, *ep.* 3.
263. *De Gr.*, book 3, c, 15; book 2, c.1.

same for a man who had eyes but was deprived of light, because it is no more physically impossible for a blind man without eyes to see than it is for one who has eyes but is without light, for physical impossibility is simply that which exceeds the natural powers. So that anyone can see how baseless is this first reply of Jansen.

2. Let us examine the second, which is still more so. He says that all the commandments are possible to man, just so far as God can give him grace to make him keep them: "All men are said to be able to believe, to be able to love God . . . for this power is nothing else than a passive flexibility of capacity, through which they are able to receive faith and charity."[264] So that, according to Jansen, man's sin in breaking the commandments is in proportion to his capacity of receiving grace to fulfill them. But by this rule we might say that the blind can see and the deaf hear because God can make them see and hear; but, for all that, it is physically impossible for the blind to see or the deaf to hear unless God gives them the power. So that to say that it is sufficient reason to call a precept possible if it is possible to man in case God gives him the power is either nonsense or fraud, intended to hide the truth; for, I ask, what help can a man have from that grace which he might have but has not at the time? It is the same as saying a man might observe all the precepts if he could observe them, but at present he cannot. When the sick man, says St. Augustine, needs care to cure him, he cannot get well without care, however he may wish it: "Nor yet can he become well when he will, but when he is healed by the use of proper care."[265]

3. Jansen's third answer is that liberty of will consists entirely in knowing the delightful object and in taking pleasure in it: "Wherefore"—these are his words—"after surveying the arguments of Augustine, on which the whole doctrine of free will depends, we think that it is nothing but knowledge and delectation, or a pleasurable complacency in the object which has the power over the freewill to make it accept or reject. . . . Concerning knowledge we are not very particular, for scarcely anyone doubts that it is necessary to an act of will."[266] So that, according to Jansen, the liberty of man consists, on the one hand, in his complacency in the

---

264. Book 3, c. 15.
265. *De Perf. Just.*, c. 3, rat. 5.
266. Book 7, c. 3.

delectation; on the other hand, in his knowledge of the object, or, in other words, in that judgment indifferent (equally applicable either to good or evil) whereby he knows the good and evil of the action; as, for instance, in murder, he knows the evil of the sin and the pleasure of the revenge. Hence he says in another place that the wicked sin in proportion as they know by means of the law the malice of sin: "The first effect of the Law is confessed to be to give the knowledge of sin."[267] And he quotes the text of St. Paul, "I did not know sin but by the law" (Romans 7:7). In this he followed Calvin, who said: "The object of the law is to render man inexcusable; and this would not be a bad definition of it: it is the knowledge of the conscience distinguishing between right and wrong, for the purpose of taking away the pretext of ignorance."[268] But we may answer that the indifferent judgment, or the knowledge of good and evil which belongs only to the intellect, can never constitute the freedom of choice which belongs altogether to the will; for liberty consists simply in the free choice of the will to do or not to do a thing.

4. Jansen gives a fourth reply, but this is more incongruous and untenable than any of the former. He says that for sin it is not requisite to have the liberty of indifference, so that a man should be free from all necessity of sinning; but that it is enough to have a liberty of exercise or of choice, so as to be able to abstain from the particular sin to which our concupiscence tempts us, but only by committing another. "So that"—these are his words—"a man may act and abstain from this particular sin, at least by committing another,"[269] whereby he places man in such a dilemma that in order to avoid one sin, he must necessarily commit another; and he says that such a liberty is sufficient to make a man guilty, though he may be necessitated to sin in one way or another. Thus he explains himself more clearly in another place: "The will of fallen man by no means ceases to be free in committing sin, although it be bound by a certain general necessity of sinning; for it will be free in its exercise (as they say), necessitated in the kind of thing it is to choose."[270] In answer to this we might repeat all that we said in chapter II, section II, p. 103, against Giovenino, who

---

267. Book 1, c. 7.
268. *Inst.*, book 2, c. 2.
269. *De St. nat. laps.*, book 4, c. 21.
270. *Ibid.*, c. 19.

says that all sinners, though deprived of sufficient grace, yet sin by this liberty of exercise. But what kind of liberty is this that a man, whether he be good or bad, could be called guilty, though he is necessitated to sin in one way or another? St. Thomas says that it is heresy to maintain that the will merits or demerits when it acts through necessity, although not compelled by violence to act: "Some have asserted that the will of man is necessarily moved to choose a thing . . . but they still did not assert that the will is forced. . . . But this opinion is heretical, for it destroys the rule of merit or demerit in human actions; for there seems to be nothing meritorious or otherwise in a man acting from necessity in a way that he cannot help."[271] Moreover, when a man is necessitated to commit one or the other sin, according to the general consent of all theologians, if he chooses the less sin, even though he voluntarily chooses it, he does not sin, because he is without the liberty which is required before an action can be imputed to him as sin. So that, in our case, when, by reason of a concupiscence that outweighs grace, a man has chosen the less of two sins, he does not sin.

But putting aside all these reflections, the direct answer is that, supposing Jansen's principle of the pleasure relatively preponderating to be true, this liberty of exercise to abstain from one sin by committing another becomes quite impossible. His principle, as we have already explained, is that when the carnal pleasure outweighs the heavenly, then the will is necessitated to consent to that individual pleasure to which it is physically drawn. And therefore he somewhere says that the superior pleasure destroys the indifference of the will; for as a weight inclines the index of a balance which before stood in equilibrium, so does the pleasure move the will to consent to that concupiscence to which it tempts it: "Since [the carnal delight] by the persuasion of its motion is the cause that the man, who before the motion was indifferent whether he acted or not, should be by the very motion of the concupiscence impelled to one side or the other, like a balance into which a weight, is put."[272] He says the same in another place, where he tries to refute those who will have it that the superior pleasure moves morally, and he says that it does not draw and determine

271. *De Mal.*, q. 6, a. un.
272. *De Gr.*, book 7, c. 14.

the will to accept the object proposed to it morally but physically: "Since that is called moral predetermination, which is only in the object when it, as it were, counsels, orders, or beseeches; but this [delectation] has its seat in the very power of the will, which it sets in motion by the intensity of the pleasure it gives, and by setting it in motion determines it; since it makes the will determine its own object, and therefore it may be said to predetermine the will."[273] So that, according to Jansen, the pleasure predetermines the will to embrace the object to which it moves it before the will determines itself. And that this is the true meaning of Jansen the learned Diroys has no doubt, who on this account says that Jansen does not differ from the astrologers, who make the will of man subject to the influence of the planets, "so that the will is determined in the choice of its object by any impression which may happen to precede its determination." The Archbishop of Vienna says the same in his book *Baianism and Jansenism Revived*: "The Jansenists contend that by a pleasure superior in degree the will is invincibly determined in its operation, without any respect to the future determination of the will itself."[274]

Granting this system, how is the liberty of exercise possible, since according to Jansen the preponderating pleasure by itself predetermines the will to accept it, so that, as in the balance the less weight necessarily gives way to the larger, so does the will necessarily yield to the preponderating pleasure. So that, for instance, if anyone is drawn by this pleasure to take another man's property, it is true that he may be led to abstain from thieving by love for his own reputation; but in cases where this love either does not exist or is not greater than the pleasure of stealing, the love of reputation certainly cannot conquer, and then evidently all liberty of exercise ceases.

REFUTATION OF THE THIRD PROPOSITION

But let us now pass on to the third proposition of Jansen: "To merit and demerit in a state of fallen nature, man does not require freedom from necessity, but freedom from compulsion." He says then that, in order to merit or to sin, the liberty of indifference, which excludes necessity, is

---

273. Book 8, c. 3.
274. *Bajan. et Jans. red.*, app. 2.

not wanted, but it is enough if the will is not repugnant. And he goes so far as to assert that it is a paradox to say that the act of will is free, so far forth as the will is at liberty to accept or refuse the object. This proposition, also condemned as heretical, follows similarly from his system; for, supposing that the will, when moved by a preponderating pleasure, must necessarily obey it, it necessarily follows (as Jansen shows) that it is sufficient for merit or demerit that a man should be willing to consent to the pleasure, although he cannot do otherwise than be willing and is even physically necessitated to be so. F. Serry well maintains that it is a monstrous doctrine to say, "Merit can coexist with the necessity of acting." And it was before this called heretical by St. Thomas, whose words, already quoted,[275] I shall be pardoned for repeating here: "Some have asserted that the will of man is necessarily moved to choose a thing; but they still did not assert that the will is forced. But this opinion is heretical, for it destroys the rule of merit and demerit in human actions; for there seems to be nothing meritorious or otherwise in a man acting from necessity in any way that he cannot help."

And with reason it is called heresy, for it is contrary to Holy Scripture: "God is faithful, who will not suffer you to be tempted above that you are able, but will also make with the temptation issue that you may be able to bear it" (1 Corinthians 10:13). But Jansen says that at times man is so completely deprived of grace that he cannot resist temptations and is necessitated to succumb to them.

Moses said to the people, "This commandment that I command you this day is not above you" (Deuteronomy 30:11). Again, "Blessed is he who could have transgressed and has not transgressed, and could do evil things and has not done them" (Sirach 31:10). Therefore it is not sufficient for merit that a man should act willingly, but it is necessary that he also act freely; that is, that he should be able to neglect the commandments, and should not be necessitated to fulfill them; and, vice versa, in sin that he should have the grace to abstain, and that it should be his own fault if he does not abstain.

Nor is the reply of the impious Theodore Beza valid here; he says that the necessity does not depend on nature but on original sin, by which

---

275. Page 114.

man voluntarily deprived himself of liberty and is therefore justly punished for sinning, though he be necessitated to sin; for it may be answered that if a servant had by his own fault broken his leg, his master would be unjust if, after having for given the fault, he commanded him to run and punished him for not running. "To hold a man guilty of sin," says St. Augustine, "because he has not done what he could not do is abominable iniquity and folly."[276]

Moreover, supposing that man could merit or demerit when acting by necessity, without any balance of power to do otherwise, I do not know how it could be reconciled with Holy Scripture, which says: "You have your choice; choose this day that which pleases you, whom you would rather serve, whether . . . the gods of the Amorites . . . but as for me and my house, we will serve the Lord" (Joshua 24:15). A choice cannot be given where men act from necessity and without liberty; so that this text clearly proves that man is free from necessity. "A full power of choosing either side," says Petavius on this passage, "is clearly shown; so that the will, as it were, suspended and placed in the middle, may choose whichever it likes of the two objects."[277]

The same is said in other parts of Scripture: "I call heaven and earth to witness this day, that I have set before you life and death, blessing and cursing. Choose, therefore, life, that both you and your seed may live" (Deuteronomy 30:19). "God made man from the beginning and left him in the hand of his own counsel. He added his commandments and precepts. . . . Before man is life and death, good and evil; that which he shall choose shall be given him" (Sirach 15:14–17). On the latter passage Petavius says: "If the teacher had now to decide the present point, how could he more clearly express the freedom from necessity which man enjoys? If he lived among us and judged from our point of view, he could not describe in more precise terms the nature and property of human liberty and of free will than he has done here.[278]

There are other texts to the same purpose: "I called, and you refused" (Proverbs 1:24). "They have been rebellious to the light" (Job 24:13). "I looked that it should bring forth grapes, and it has brought forth wild

276. *De Duab. an.*, c. 12.
277. *De Op. sex d.*, book 3, c. 2.
278. *Loco sup. cit.*

grapes" (Isaiah 5:2). "You always resist the Holy Spirit" (Acts 7:53). It is certainly the work of the Holy Spirit to call men, to enlighten their minds, and to move the will to good; but how can it be said that he refuses the call that he rebels against the light, that he resists grace, who is destitute of preponderating grace and therefore must necessarily yield to the prevailing concupiscence?

II.   True doctrine of St. Augustine on the "victorious delectation" and on free will

"But what," says Jansen, "if Augustine before me has maintained this same theory, that we must necessarily do that which pleases us most, according to the well known passage, 'It is necessary that we act according to that which delights us most'?"[279] Now, before we answer Jansen, we must premise that St. Augustine, who had to confute several heresies of his time, all on the subject of grace and all contrary to one another, had to speak of it diffusely and upon different points of view, and is therefore in several places obscure. Hence it has come to pass that not only each of the Catholic schools boasts of having him on its side, though their opinions are quite different, but also Calvin and Jansen, whose errors have been condemned by the Church, have presumed to call him their patron. Calvin, writing against Pighius, says, "We follow nothing but Augustine. . . . Pighius may squeak as he pleases, he will never make us allow that Augustine is not on our side."[280] And Jansen puts forward Augustine as his sole teacher, so that he even called his book by the title of *Augustinus*. And the Jansenists only call themselves Augustinians. From these premises we only wish to infer that many passages of St. Augustine require explanation by comparison with other passages of his works, where he declares his true opinion, if we would not be misled. Now let us come to the point.

We have already explained at the beginning of the chapter that this sentence of St. Augustine ought not and cannot be understood of indeliberate pleasure, antecedent to any cooperation of the will, but ought to

---

279.   *In Gal.*, n. 49.
280.   *Adv. Pigh.*, book 3.

be understood of deliberate and consequent pleasure; for in cases where man freely consents to the pleasure, then, certainly, it is necessary that he should act upon it. And this is proved by what Augustine says in other places, where he confounds pleasure with love, or, rather, explains that the superior pleasure is nothing else than that deliberate love, and that affection, which, by our own free choice, predominates in us; in which pleasure, if we deliberately take delight, then it is necessary that we act upon it. So that in substance, he simply says that the will must act upon that which it deliberately loves the most; for in one place he says that the pleasure is, as it were, the weight of the soul, which drags it along with it—"for pleasure is, as it were, the weight of the soul"[281]—and in another place that this weight which draws each man's soul is his love: "My love is my weight."[282] This he explains more clearly in another place, where he says we ought to be careful, "by God's help, to be so disposed as not to be tripped up by inferior things, and to take pleasure only in the higher things."[283] See how clearly he speaks of deliberate pleasure, freely accepted. In another place: "What is it to be drawn by pleasure? To delight in the Lord; and he will give you the petitions of your heart" (Psalm 37:4). Again, "See how the Father draws! He delights us by teaching, not by laying us under necessity."[284] Again, "If we wish to enjoy the pleasures of heaven, we must bridle unlawful pleasure; as when we fast, the appetite rises against us; this it does by pleasure [i.e., indeliberate], but we restrain it by the law of the governing reason."[285] So that, according to St. Augustine, the pleasure which incites us to break the law may be freely repressed by man by means of the dominant reason, and by the help of grace. Hence he exhorts us, "Let justice so delight you as to conquer even lawful pleasures."[286]

This is made still clearer by the context of the passage on which we are now disputing, where, after saying, "We must needs act upon the greater pleasure," he adds, "It is clear that our life must be according to our pur-

---

281. *De Mus.*, book 6, c. 11.
282. *Conf.*, book 13, c. 9.
283. *De Mus.*, book 6, c. 11.
284. *In Joan.*, tr. 26.
285. *De Serm. Dom. in monte*, book 1, c. 12.
286. Serm. 159, E. B.

suits, and our pursuits must be according to our affections [mark this]. Therefore, if there are two contradictory things, the command of justice and the carnal habit, and both of them are loved, we shall pursue that which we love most."[287] So that when he says we must needs act according to that which delights us most, he only means that the will must necessarily act on that which it loves best; nor will it do to say, with Jansen, that what gives most pleasure is most loved; for this is not always true, and St. Augustine expressly contradicts it when, in his *Confessions*, he says of himself, "I did not do that in which my affections took incomparably more pleasure, and which as soon as I would, I could do,"[288] by which he means that he was already moved by God with an indeliberate affection, which made virtue incomparably more pleasant to him than vice, and that he might easily have been virtuous if he would, but that he resisted grace and refused to be virtuous, and abandoned him self to vice.

Further, if St. Augustine had believed that it was necessary for us to act upon the greater pleasure, he could never have said, "When the unlawful pleasure of concupiscence tickles you, fight, resist, do not consent; and the saying is fulfilled, 'Do not go after your desires'" (Sirach 18:30).[289] Still further, he says elsewhere that of two persons who have the same temptation to impurity, it sometimes happens that one consents to it, and the other resists. And why? Because, he says, one wills to observe chastity, the other wills not: "If both are tempted by the same [mark the word "same"] temptation, and one yields and consents to it, while the other perseveres, what else is shown but that one willed to fail, the other willed not to fail in chastity?"[290]

Moreover, when he says that it is necessary that we should act upon that which best pleases us, it may be asked whether he speaks of deliberate or indeliberate pleasure. Now, we say that if he had meant indeliberate pleasure, he would have been obliged in consequence to deny that the will, in order to be truly free, need be free not only from violence but also from necessity. But there are a thousand places where he teaches the reverse and says that man, whether in good or in evil, acts without

---

287. *In Gal.*, n. 54.
288. *Conf.*, book 8, c. 8.
289. Serm. 155, E. B.
290. *De Civ. D.*, book 12, c. 6.

necessity; therefore, when he speaks of the predominant pleasure overcoming, he must necessarily mean the deliberate or consequent pleasure. To quote a few of these numerous passages:

"Our will would be no will at all if it were not in our own power; for that is not free to us which we have not in our power."[291]

In another place, speaking of the passage of St. Matthew where our Lord talks of good fruit springing from a good tree and bad fruit from a bad tree (Matthew 7:17), he says, "When, therefore, our Lord says this—do this or do that—he shows that it is in the power of man to do it; for he that will not keep the law can keep it if he will."[292] Calvin objects that Augustine is here speaking of man in the state of innocence; but Bellarmine well observes that St. Augustine is here explaining a passage where our Lord is speaking against the Jews and says of them, "You shall know them by their fruits." So that it can never be supposed that St. Augustine meant to apply the remark to Adam. Moreover, he repeats what he had said against the Manichees when writing against the Pelagians: "Whenever it is said, 'Do not this and do not that,' and whenever an act of will is required of us to do or not to do something which God commands or forbids, in such places the will is shown to be sufficiently free."[293] Here Jansen replies (like a partisan of Calvin, as he is) that St. Augustine is speaking of necessity violently imposed on us, not of simple necessity. But here again Jansen is mistaken; for on this point St. Augustine agreed with the Pelagians and conceded to them that the will was free both from coercive and from simple necessity; hence in his book against Julian, he did not scruple to say: "Both of us affirm that the will in man is free. But you say that anyone is free to do good without God's help; hence you are a Pelagian."[294] When St. Augustine says, "Both of us affirm," he admitted the same liberty to do or not to do which the Pelagians maintained, and they certainly maintained it to be exempt from any necessity whatever; so that there is no doubt that he held the will to be free not only from violence, but from any necessity whatever; he only contradicted the Pelagians in this point that they maintained the will to be free to do good even without grace.

---

291. *De Lib. Arb.*, book 3, c. 3.
292. *De act. cum Fel. man.*, book 2, c. 4.
293. *De Gr. et Lib. Arb.*, c. 2.
294. *De Nupt. et Conc.*, book 2, c. 3.

Further, St. Augustine says that it is difficult to reconcile the liberty of the will with the efficacy of grace: "This question, wherein we discuss the choice of the will and the grace of God, is so difficult to determine that when we defend free will, we seem to deny the grace of God; and when we assert the grace of God, we are supposed to destroy free will."[295] If St. Augustine had supposed that the will was not free from simple necessity, but only from violence, it would not have been difficult, but the easiest thing possible, to understand how grace acted; when, therefore, he said that it was difficult to understand, it was because he held that efficacious grace certainly produced its effect in good acts; and, on the other hand, that the will did these acts freely, working without any necessity to prevent it from being able to do or to wish any acts different from those to which it was moved by grace. For the rest, the holy Father held it as certain that man, with the help of ordinary grace, was able to fulfill the commandments or, at any rate, to procure by prayer greater help to enable him to fulfill them; otherwise (as he said), God would not have imposed these commandments on him: "Nor would he have commanded us to do this if he had considered it impossible to be done by man."[296]

We will quote some more passages of St. Augustine where he reiterates the doctrine that the will of man is free from any necessity: "For that would not be sin which was not done by the will; and therefore punishment would also be unjust if man had not free will; that is, if he acted well or ill through necessity."[297] Again, "Who would not exclaim that it is folly to give commands to a man who is not free to do what is commanded, and that it is injustice to condemn the man who had no power to fulfill the command?"[298] Again, "If the motion whereby the will turns aside from the unchangeable good is natural and necessary, it can by no means be culpable."[299] Then, after saying that previous grace is necessary to enable us to do good, he adds, "But to consent to the call of God, or to dissent from it, is in the power of our own will."[300] Here he plainly teaches

---

295. *De Gr. Chr.*, c. 47.
296. *In Ps. lvi.*
297. *De Lib. Arb.*, book 2, c. 1.
298. *De Fide cont. Man.*, c. 10.
299. *De Lib. Arb.*, book 3, c. 1.
300. *De Sp. et Litt.*, c. 34.

that the will can freely obey grace or resist it. Nor does it avail to say with Jansen that St. Augustine only means that to consent and dissent is the proper office of the will; for we can never believe that the holy Doctor would have taken such useless pains to prove that consent and dissent belong to the will and not to the intellect, a thing which any illiterate man can tell. Especially as St. Augustine's words, just before the last quoted sentence, are as follows: "No one has it in his power to determine what shall come into his mind, but to consent, etc." So that it is clear that he is speaking of the free power of the will to consent or dissent from that which comes into the head. In another place he says, "No one but God can make the tree" (he is speaking of the good trees that produce good fruit and of the bad trees which produce bad fruit), "but every man's will has power to choose either good or bad. When, therefore, our Lord says, 'Do this,' or 'Do that,' he shows that it is in men's power to choose what to do." Elsewhere, in explanation of the help *sine quo*, he says, "Without it the will cannot will; but still it is left to the free will either to will or not to will, to use the help or not to use it."

From all this it is very clearly seen how far St Augustine was from the opinion of Jansen, that the will of man in its action is not free from necessity, much less that it is obliged to follow the preponderating pleasure, which by its impulse invincibly moves and determines it.

III. Continuation of the refutation of Jansen and of his adherents

Now, let us apply this to the point we have in view, namely, to prove that God gives everyone either proximate grace or the remote grace of prayer to enable him to observe the precepts; since otherwise the transgression of the law could never be imputed to him as a fault. Let us then see what are the two propositions that are exactly opposite to those of Jansen.

His first is, "Some precepts of God are impossible to the just man who wishes and tries to fulfill them with his present strength; nor does God give him grace to make them possible." Hence the Catholic proposition, contradictory of this, is as follows: "Not any of the precepts of God is impossible, at least to the just man who wishes to observe them, and who endeavors to do so; nor, even with his present strength, is he without the grace (either proximate, or at least remote) whereby he may at least obtain greater assistance to enable him to fulfill them." And here we must again observe that, to avoid the condemned error it, is not enough to grant the absolute possibility of observing the precept, for the Jansenists themselves admit this possibility; but we must also admit the possibility (relatively to the actual carnal delectation which preponderates over the delectation of grace) to fulfill the commandment when it is incumbent on us to do so, or at least to obtain grace to keep it; since the error of Jansen consists precisely in denying not the absolute, but the relative, possibility.

Jansen third proposition is that "in order to merit ill or well in the state of fallen nature, man need not have freedom from necessity, but only freedom from compulsion." Hence the Catholic proposition is the contradictory: To merit ill or well, even in the state of fallen nature, man, whether just or unjust, requires freedom, not only from compulsion, but also from simple necessity; since, according to the Catholic doctrine, the voluntary, whenever it is necessary, is not free in such a sense as is sufficient to merit ill or well in this life; but to merit ill or well the will must be free from any necessity whatever of being obliged to consent to either of two things determinately.

Moreover, F. Fortunato da Brescia (a man universally celebrated by the learned of these days, especially by Muratori), in his late work entitled *Confutation of the System of Cornelius Jansen*, says that if this system could possibly be true, God's law would be either foolish or unjust; for, according to it, if the heavenly pleasure predominates, then the will, quite independently of the law, is obliged to follow the precise impulse of the pleasure, and thus the law is useless; or, if the earthly pleasure predominates, then the law is unjust, for God imposes a commandment which it is physically impossible for man to obey, since the will must necessarily yield to the temptation.

And in this way all the threats and admonitions of the Scriptures would be useless, and there would be no human action which could merit reward or punishment, since all the actions of man would be done through necessity. So that whenever anyone exhorted us to do well, we might answer with Eusebius against the Fatalists, "These powers are not mine, O Doctor; for they will do it if the fates so desire [i.e., if the carnal delight does not preponderate] that which is fated will necessarily come to pass."[301] I must necessarily follow the pleasure that prevails.

The same author says further that if we admit this system, we must also admit Manicheism, which supposed two principles, a good and an evil; and says that as all the acts of men were derived from one or the other principle, the man was obliged to follow that which prevailed. Nor does it do to say that the necessity in the system of the preponderating pleasure is not derived from a good or evil principle, as the Manicheans held, but depends on the sin of Adam, which is its cause; for the question is not through what principle the will acts necessarily when it is moved, but whether the will after Adam's fall has remained free from necessity in its actions. And this is what the Jansenists deny, who hold that the will merits well and ill, though it is necessitated to will that to which the preponderating pleasure determines it. But, as F. Fortunate well observes, the books of Arnold, Irenee, Ventrochio, and the other Jansenists were condemned for this very error of maintaining Jansen's principle of the invincibility of the pleasure which is superior in degree. And we know that it was for this reason that the theology of Giovenino was prohibited; for though he did not expressly hold the system we are discussing, yet he imprudently spoke too obscurely on the point: "The physical nature of efficacious grace consists simply in the preponderance of the pleasure which the mind takes in goodness."[302] Still he did not use the phrase "relatively preponderating," though he proves his proposition by the often-quoted text of St. Augustine, "We must act according to that which pleases us most." And for this cause his work was so long prohibited and has at last been allowed because of the addition of a compendium, entitled *The True Doctrine of the Church*, extracted from the theology of Tourneley, who has amply and well confuted the system.

F. Fortunate concludes: "It is clear, then, that the system of Jansen is favorable to them [Luther and Calvin], and so cannot be maintained by a Catholic without violating his faith. For we cannot preserve our faith and religion while defending a system on the admission of whose

---

301. *Praep. ev.*, book 6, c. 6.
302. *Instit.*, p. 6, d. 1, q. 4, c. 7.

fundamental principles the reception of condemned doctrines necessarily follows." Tourneley meant the same when he said, "Since the Church condemned the five propositions in the sense of Jansen, they must be condemned as parts of Jansen's theory of the superior and relatively preponderating pleasure, which is the foundation of his whole system."[303]

Nor will it avail to say that the system of Jansen is one thing, which supposes that the pleasure which relatively preponderates is indeliberate, that is, that it comes to us without any assent of the will; but that it is quite a different thing to say that the pleasure, though it relatively preponderates by the superiority of its degree, yet is deliberate; that is, it preponderates not by itself and by its own strength (as the maintainers of this system say), but it preponderates by being reinforced by the power of the consenting will. And hence they say that though the preponderating pleasure certainly and infallibly overcomes, yet it does not do so necessarily, as Jansen maintained.

This will not avail because, as Tourneley well replies, that grace or that pleasure which is infallibly efficacious, and invincibly determines the will by its preponderating power, cannot but necessitate the will to consent. And he proves it thus: "That grace necessitates which supposes the will to be destitute of real power to resist it; but of this nature is grace, which is infallibly efficacious because of the superiority of the degree of its strength. For grace of this kind supposes that the will has only inferior strength to resist; but it is a contradiction to say that superior strength, acting as such, can be overcome by inferior; otherwise it would be necessary that the inferior strength should act beyond the degree of its power of acting." Nor does it avail to reply that though the power of grace relatively preponderating is superior to that of the concupiscence taken by itself, it is not superior to that of the concupiscence joined with that of the will, because, as Tourneley says, such a power of the will could only be admitted with respect to evil which a man can do by himself, as when he overcomes one vice by another, or at least with respect to good of the natural order—but not with respect to supernatural good, such as the conquest of a strong concupiscence, which cannot be effected without God's grace.

---

303. *De Gr. Chr.*, q. 3, *in prop. 5 Jans.*

Hence the Fathers of Diospolis required every Pelagian, among other things, "to confess that when we fight against temptations and unlawful concupiscence, the victory comes not from our own will, but from the help of God."[304] And the reason is, as St. Thomas teaches, that no active principle can produce an effect exceeding the sphere of its activity; so that no natural principle or cause can produce a supernatural effect: "No act exceeds the proportion of its active principle; and hence we see that in natural things, nothing can by its own operation produce an effect which exceeds the power of its activity, but can only by its own operation produce an effect proportionate to its power."[305] So that the natural power of the human will, although united to the power of grace, cannot, when the latter is inferior to the power of the concupiscence, contribute to produce a supernatural effect, such as the conquest of a violent concupiscence that preponderates over grace. And, in fact, the Jansenists say, we are contented if you grant to us that the delectation certainly overcomes by reason of its superior power. See how one of them, the Abbot de Bourzeis, speaks: "It is sufficient for us if this single truth be granted, that as often as we consent to the grace of God, it always arises from the right love which God inspires, being superior in strength to the perverse love; and in consequence of this superiority always most certainly overcoming it."[306] Hence Tourneley, speaking of the two systems, of pleasure absolutely preponderating and of pleasure relatively preponderating, concludes: "We have known orthodox theologians who test efficacious grace by its pleasure being absolutely and simply preponderating over all other pleasures, and who call that sufficient grace which has just power enough to overcome the lust actually opposed to it. But we have only met with Jansenists who maintain that no grace can overcome unless it is relatively preponderating in degree, and who admit no other sufficient grace than one that is inferior in strength to the superior concupiscence which opposes it."[307]

So that, to conclude, we do not intend now to blame the opinion that the will, even when it follows the greater delectation, yet always acts

---

304. *Cath. conf.*
305. *Summa,* 1.2, q. 109, a. 5.
306. *Collat.* 4, c. 30.
307. *De Gr. Chr.,* q. 9, a. 2, obj. 6.

freely, that is, without necessity, and with true power (not merely nominal or hypothetical power) to act in a contrary way; but we only reject the opinion of those who say that when one of the two pleasures, the carnal or the heavenly, preponderates by being greater in degree than the other, then man has no more power to resist and to overcome it, because the greater force always overcomes the less.

Nevertheless, I cannot in this place neglect to mention the difficulty that I find in this system of the preponderating delectation. Its defenders say, as also F. John Laurence Berti, that the efficacy of grace, as they maintain it, does not differ in substance from the efficacy as taught by the Thomists, though founded on different principles; for the Thomists make the efficacy of grace consist in a physical predetermination, but the Jansenists in the preponderating pleasure. That which is done by physical premonition, according to the Thomists, the same is done by victorious delectation according to the Augustinians: namely, the liberty of the will is moved to give consent *in actu secundo*. Further, both opinions teach that man still has the power, *in actu primo*, to act in opposite directions, so that the will always acts freely and without necessity.[308]

But I observe that, as the principles and the reasons of these two opinions are different, so also are their consequences.

According to the Thomists, the reason of the efficacy of grace is because the created will is in a state of passive potentiality, able to receive the motions of grace; so that to come to actual operation it must be moved by God, as the first agent and first free cause, who, by his predetermination, adapts and determines the potentiality (of the will) into actuality. This only relates to the act; but as for the power of capability, the Thomists say that man has the grace of potentiality wholly complete and in proximate preparation so as to be able to act virtuously. Thus F. Gonet: "The grace which gives the power gives the full complement, and all the strength or sufficiency which is requisite, so far as the *actus*

---

308. Berti. *August. Syst. Vindic. Diss.* 5, c. 3, n. 4. "*In actu primo*," "*in actu secundo*." "*In actu primo*" is much the same with our English expression "in power" or "in liability"; "*in actu secundo*," in act. Thus, at every moment we are subject to concupiscence *in actu primo* because we are liable to be tempted by passion to disobey God's will; but we are only subject to it "*in actu secundo*" when we are at this moment tempted by passion to disobey God's will.—*Ed.*

primus is concerned."[309] So also Cardinal Gotti: "Sufficient grace gives proximate power, and complete power within the limits of potentiality."[310] And thus all other Thomists in general; and if any of them apparently speak otherwise, it is only of the *actus secundus*, not *primus*.

On the other hand, the reason of the principle of those who maintain the opinion of the pleasure superior in degree is because (as they say) whereas at first, in the state of innocence, man only required "sufficient grace" to do well, since his will, being then sound and in perfect balance, could easily act with only sufficient grace without needing efficacious grace, now, on the other hand, since the fall of Adam, the will, being injured and inclined to evil, has need of "efficacious grace," which, by means of the victorious pleasure, adapts it for acting virtuously. But (I say), according to this reason for the system, granting that the will of man has become so weak that, in its present state, it cannot act without efficacious grace, it is impossible to say that man still has, by virtue of sufficient grace, not even in the *actus primus*, nor either in the *sensus coinpositus*, nor *sensus divisus*, the complete and proximately prepared power to observe the commandments or to be able to do any good work, even though it be mediate, by means of which he can place himself in a position to obtain greater help to enable him to fulfill the law.

I know that the supporters of this opinion have no objection to grant this and to say that, in our present state, sufficient grace does not give complete and prepared power. "Sufficient grace," says F. Macedo, one of this school, "does not give power proximately complete and prepared." And elsewhere, speaking of the grace of Adam innocent and of Adam fallen, he says, "The first supposed [a power] prepared and free; the second a power crippled, hindered, and enslaved."[311]

So supposing that grace, when inferior to the concupiscence, does not give complete and prepared power to observe the commandments, it

---

309. *Man. Thom.*, tr. 7, c. 10.
310. *De Gr.*, q. 2, d. 4, 2. Gotti, vol. 2, tr. 7. *De Grat.*, q. 2, *dub.* 4, n. 4, p. 286. "*In sensu composito*," "*in sensu diviso.*" The meaning of these phrases will best be shown by illustrations. I have full moral power to avoid all venial sins "*in sensu diviso*"—that is, I can avoid each one of them; there is no one which I cannot avoid, but not "*in sensu composito*," for I have not moral power to avoid all venial sins collectively.—*Ed.*
311. *Cort. D. Aug.*, tr. 2, q. 3, a. 2.

can in truth be no longer called sufficient. So that, in fact, F. Berti, who defends such a system of the relatively victorious delectation, finds no difficulty in further granting that such inferior grace ought properly to be called inefficacious and not sufficient. So that on this system, they who do not receive from God grace that is efficacious, by means of the delectation relatively victorious over that of the concupiscence, have not even grace sufficient to enable them to fulfill the commandments. F. Berti thus writes in defense of his opinion. First, he states the three objections of his opponents, which are as follows: "There are three things which savor of the Jansenist dogma and are the fountain and source of the five condemned propositions; to which the new Jansenists, the chief of whom are two (doubtless pretended) Augustinians, make no objection." (These two are F. Bellelli and F. Berti, against whom the Archbishop of Vienna wrote.) "The first of these three things is that they do not make efficacious grace consist simply in a victorious delectation, but in a delectation relatively preponderating, etc. The second is that they deny the existence of a power proximately prepared in the case of a delectation of a lower grade, requiring for this, as regards the power and the *actus primus*, a stronger delectation; and therefore inefficacious grace (or the assistance *sine quo*, which they preach about) is not really sufficient grace, either in the Molinist sense or the Thomist sense; since sufficient grace, by the common consent of Catholics, confers power proximately prepared. The third thing that follows from this is that they deny the existence of such a thing as sufficient grace, the very name of which they fraudulently abstain from using and call it rather inefficacious than insufficient." Such are the objections. Now for F. Berti's answer: "I most firmly and unhesitatingly declare that the three doctrines just cited are no way erroneous, nor principles of the five condemned propositions; but that some people, moved indeed by a laudable zeal for refuting Jansen, but nevertheless carried away by the prejudice of their private judgment, have made no distinction between what is Catholic and what is erroneous and condemned; and that from these people's lucubrations, some anonymous sciolist [the Archbishop of Vienna, to wit] and some other men of scanty learning and fat wits have taken occasion to calumniate the unshaken doctrines of Augustine (which, whether they admit it or not, are the same as ours) as monstrous heresies."[312]

Now I confess myself also to be precisely one of these scantily learned and gross-minded men; for I cannot understand how the propositions of F. Berti hold together, since in their consequences they appear clearly repugnant to one another. If he had said that toob serve the divine law we have need of efficacious grace, but that sufficient grace, which is given to all, gives the proximate power to enable us to pray, and by prayer to obtain the greater assistance necessary for the actual observance of the commandments, we should quite agree; for this is our opinion, which we shall set forth and prove in the next chapter.

But we cannot agree, because while speaking of prayer he says well that every one of the faithful, by means of this sufficient grace, if he puts no impediment in the way, can pray, and by prayer obtain the immediate assistance to enable him actually to fulfill the commandments. "To each of the faithful"—these are his words—"unless he freely puts an obstacle in the way, the grace of prayer is given, by which he may obtain the aid immediately sufficient to fulfill the commandments."[313] And, further, he says in another place that the said sufficient grace, common to all the faithful, although only remotely sufficient for the observance of the precepts, is nevertheless proximately sufficient for prayer, by which efficacious grace is then obtained: "In him who has the little will [that is, the will which is furnished by the sufficient grace], there is a power proximately sufficient for prayer and remotely sufficient for the observance of the commandments, which he will be able proximately to fulfill when, by prayer, he has obtained a strong will" (which strong will is furnished by efficacious grace).[314] He says then, and says wisely, that for the observance of the commandments, it cannot be said that sufficient grace gives to all the proximate power actually to fulfill them; for (as he well observes in the place just cited, s. 4) the proximate power to observe the precepts is that which needs nothing further to enable it to act; hence he writes in the same section 4, near the beginning, that the complete and prepared power can only be had from efficacious grace: "Efficacious grace alone

312. Aug. syst. Vind., d. 4, c. 1, s. 2.
313. *De Theol. Disc.*, book 18, c. 8, p 4.
314. *Aug. syst. vind.*, d. 4, c. 1, s. 9.

gives the complete and ready power." Hence he adds that, in order that the sufficient grace may be said to be proximately sufficient for actual operation, "it is requisite that it should not need any further means in order to act." So that, according to the reasoning of F. Berti, though the sufficient grace does not supply all the faithful with proximate power to keep the commandments, yet it supplies all with power proximately sufficient to pray. Therefore each of the faithful, by the aid of "sufficient grace" alone, can actually pray, without the need of any further assistance, that is, of efficacious grace.

But then I do not know how this agrees with what he says in another place: "No one without grace, efficacious in itself, has the power of praying united with the act."[315] Therefore, according to this second proposition, the "sufficient grace" does not give really, but only in name, the power proximately sufficient for prayer. It only gives the power remotely sufficient if there is need of efficacious grace to make the power of praying issue in act. Either, therefore, for actual prayer, "efficacious grace" is requisite, and then it cannot be said that the sufficient grace gives the power proximately sufficient; or else "sufficient grace" gives the power proximately sufficient for actual prayer; and then there is no need of the efficacious grace of the preponderating pleasure, which he seeks to establish. But St. Augustine also, says F. Berti, requires an overpowering pleasure to enable us to pray: "Augustine teaches that, for prayer, a certain knowledge is requisite and an overpowering pleasure." I have examined the passage referred to, which is as follows: "Let us understand, if we can, that the good Lord God sometimes does not give even to his saints either the certain knowledge of some good work or an overpowering delight in it, in order that they may understand that the light wherewith their darkness is enlightened comes not from themselves but from him, and so also the sweetness by which their land yields its fruit."[316] St. Augustine does not say that an overpowering delight is requisite for prayer; he only says that sometimes God does not give even to his saints either the certain knowledge or the overpowering delight of some just work, in order that they may know that from him,

---

315. *De Theol. Disc.*, book 18, c. 8, p. 5.
316. *De Pecc. mer.*, book 2, c. 19.

and not from themselves, they have the light to illumine them, and the sweetness to make them bear fruit.

Therefore St. Augustine does not here primarily speak of the sufficient grace by which a man can work, but does not always work; nor does he say that man with only sufficient grace, and without efficacious grace, cannot actually pray; but he speaks only of efficacious grace, which, by means of an overpowering delight, infallibly causes him to do well. Secondly, he does not speak here of prayer but of just works, which properly means the observance of the precepts or of the counsels; since prayer, though it is a good work, of its own nature is not a work, but the means of obtaining the aid necessary to execute good works.

We also hold, as we said before, that efficacious grace is necessary for the observance of the commandments; but we say that for actual prayer, whereby we may obtain efficacious grace, the sufficient grace which God gives to all the faithful is enough. And thus we do no violence to the truth that God's commandments are not impossible to anyone; since every man, by means of the sufficient grace only, can perform such an easy thing as prayer; and by means of prayer he will obtain the assistance of gratuitous efficacious grace, which is necessary for the actual performance of difficult things such as the observance of the commandments. Thus says Cardinal Noris, whose words I will quote in the next chapter, and before him St. Augustine: "By the fact that we most firmly believe that God does not command impossibilities, we are admonished in easy matters what to do and in difficult matters what to ask for."[317] Otherwise, if sufficient grace were not enough for actual prayer, and the addition of efficacious grace were always necessary, and if this were denied to any man as, in fact, efficacious grace is denied to many, I cannot see how the commandments of God could be said to be possible to such a person, and how God could demand of him the observance of his law (at the time when he denies him even the efficacious grace to enable him actually to pray), and how with justice he could condemn him to hell for not observing it. This is precisely that which made Jansen say that some precepts were impossible even from the first, because he erroneously said that some men want the grace to make the precepts possible to them. But

---

317. *De Nat. et Gr.*, c. 69.

it is not so, because God gives to all men (we are not here considering the case of infidels and obstinate sinners) the proximate grace to enable them actually to pray, as we shall prove in the next chapter. And so no one will be able to make the excuse that the observance of the precepts was impossible to him; for though he had not efficacious grace for their actual observance, he had, nevertheless, grace proximately sufficient for actual prayer, by means of which he would have obtained from God efficacious grace, according to his promise of hearing whoever prays to him; and with this he certainly might have observed the precepts. And the Council of Trent has expressly declared this against Luther, who asserted that the observance of God's law was impossible even to the faithful. "God," it says, "does not command impossibilities; but by commanding, he admonishes you to do what you can and to ask for what you cannot do; and by his help he enables you to do it."[318]

---

318. Sess. 6, c. 11.

God Gives All Men the Grace to Pray if They Choose, as the "Sufficient Grace" Which Is Common to All Men Is by Itself Enough for Prayer

I. The principal theologians who teach this doctrine

Assuming, then, that God wills all men to be saved, and that, as far as he is concerned, he gives to all the graces necessary for their salvation, we must say that all men have given to them the grace to enable them actually to pray (without needing a further grace), and by prayer to obtain all further aid necessary for the observance of the commandments and for salvation. But it must be remarked that when we say, "without needing a further grace," we do not mean that the common grace gives the power of prayer without the aid of assisting grace, since, in order to exercise any act of piety, besides the exciting grace, there is doubtless required the assisting or cooperating grace. But we mean that the common grace gives every man the power of actual prayer, without a further preventing grace, which, physically or morally, determines the will of man to exercise the act of prayer. We will first mention the names of the famous theologians who teach this opinion as certain, and then we will prove it by authorities and arguments.

It is held by Isambert, Cardinal du Perron, Alphonsus le Moyne, and others whom we shall presently quote, and at greater length as a set proposition by Honoratus Tourneley. All these authors prove that every man, by means of the ordinary sufficient grace alone, can actually pray, without need of further aid, and by prayer can obtain all the graces requisite for the performance of the most difficult things.

It was also held by Cardinal Noris, who proves the proposition that man, when the commandment urges (*urgendo il precetto*), can pray if he will; and he proves it thus: "It is clear that the power to pray should be proximate in the just man or the faithful; for if the faithful has only a remote power for a simple act of prayer (I am not here speaking of fervid prayer), he will not have another proximate power to obtain the grace of prayer, otherwise the series would be infinite."[319] Assuming that in order to keep the commandments and to be saved prayer is necessary, as we proved in the beginning when we spoke of the necessity of prayer, this learned author says well that everyone has the proximate power of prayer, in order that by prayer he may obtain the proximate power to do good; and therefore all can pray with only the ordinary grace, without other assistance. Otherwise, if in order to obtain the proximate power for the act of prayer we required another power, we should still want another power of grace to obtain this power, and so on *ad infinitum*, and it would no longer be in the power of man to cooperate in his salvation.

The same author in another place maintains this doctrine more clearly: "Even in the state of fallen nature the assistance *sine quo* [i.e., the sufficient grace which is common to all] is given, though Jansen denies it; and this assistance produces in us weak acts, namely, prayer not very fervid, for fulfilling the commandments; but for the actual observance of these, the assistance *sine quo* is only a remote help, by which we can, however, obtain by prayer the assistance *quo*, or efficacious grace, by which the commandments are fulfilled."[320] So that Cardinal Noris held it as certain that in the present state all men have the assistance *sine quo*, i.e., ordinary grace, which, without need of further assistance, produces prayer, by which we can then obtain efficacious grace to enable us to observe the law. And hence we can easily understand the axiom universally received in the schools: "To him who does what in him lies, God does not refuse his grace." That is, to the man who prays and thus makes good use of the sufficient grace which enables him to do such an easy thing as prayer, God

---

319. *Jans. err. cal. Subl.*, c. 2, s. 1.
320. *Jans. err. cal. Subl.*, c. 2.

does not refuse the efficacious grace to enable him to execute difficult things. Thus, also, Louis Thomassin, who expresses astonishment at those who say that "sufficient assistance" is not enough to do any actual good work, nor to avoid any sin: "For if," he says, "this assistance is truly assistance, and gives proximate power, how is it that, out of the innumerable quantity of men who are thus assisted, none keep the commandments? Or how is it truly sufficient, if, besides it, efficacious grace is necessary? That man has not a sufficient power who wants a necessary assistance which is not in his own power."[321] He means that "sufficient grace," to be really sufficient, ought to give a man the proximate and ready power to execute a good act; but since, in order to perform such an act, another grace, namely, efficacious grace is wanted, unless a man has (at least mediately) this efficacious grace which is necessary for salvation, how can it be said that the "sufficient grace" gives this proximate and ready power? Since, says St. Thomas, "God does not neglect to do that which is necessary to salvation."[322] On the one hand, it is true that God is not bound to give us his grace, because what is *gratis* is not of obligation; but, on the other hand, supposing that he gives us commandments, he is obliged to give us the assistance necessary for observing them. And as God obliges us actually to observe every precept whenever it applies, so ought he also actually to supply us (at least mediately or remotely) with the assistance necessary for the observance of the precept, without the necessity of a further grace which is not common to all. Hence Thomassin concludes that in order to reconcile the proposition that "sufficient grace" is enough for a man's salvation with the statement that efficacious grace is requisite to observe the whole law, it is necessary to say that sufficient grace is enough to pray and to perform similar easy acts, and that by means of these we then obtain efficacious grace to fulfill the difficult acts. And this is without doubt in conformity with the doctrine of St. Augustine, who teaches, "By the very fact that God is most firmly believed not to command impossibilities, we are admonished both what to do in easy things, and in difficult things what to ask for."[323] On this passage Cardinal Noris observes, "Therefore, we are able to do easy or less perfect works

321. *Cons. sch. de gr.*, tr. 3, c. 8.
322. *Summa*, p. 1, q. 49. a. 2.
323. *De Nat. et Gr.*, c. 69.

without asking God for further help; for which, however, we must pray in more difficult works."[324] Thomassin also brings forward the authority of St. Bonaventure, Scotus, and others on this subject, and says, "All these considered the sufficient grace to be truly sufficient, whether the will consents to it or not."[325] And this he demonstrates in four parts of his book, adducing the authorities of the schoolmen for a long series of years, beginning from the year 1100.

Habert, Bishop of Vabres and Doctor of the Sorbonne, who was the first to write against Jansen, says: "We think, first that sufficient grace has only a contingent or mediate connection with the actual effect of the complete consent. . . . We think, further, that sufficient grace is a grace that disposes for efficacious grace, since from a good use of it God afterward grants to the created will the grace that performs the complete effect."[326] He had said before, "All Catholic Doctors, of all schools, have professed and do profess that a real inward grace is given, which is capable of persuading the will to consent to good, though, on account of the free resistance of the will, it sometimes does not persuade it thus to consent,"[327] and for this doctrine be quotes Gamaches, Duval, Isambert, Perez, Le Moyne, and others. Then he goes on: "The assistance, therefore, of sufficient grace disposes us for the reception of efficacious grace and is in some sort efficacious, namely, of an incomplete effect, obtained first remotely, then more nearly, and at last proximately, such as is an act of faith, hope, love, and, mixed with these, one of prayer. Hence the famous Alphonsus Le Moyne taught that this sufficient grace was the grace of asking, or of prayer, of which St. Augustine so often speaks."[328] So that, according to Habert, the difference between efficacious and sufficient grace is that the former produces its effect completely, while the latter produces it either contingently (i.e., sometimes, but not always) or mediately (i.e., by means of prayer). Moreover, he says that sufficient grace, according to the good use we make of it, prepares us to obtain efficacious grace; hence he calls sufficient grace "in

---

324. *Loco sup. cit.*
325. *Cons. sch.*, p. 2, at the end.
326. *Theol. Gr. Patr.*, book 2, c. 15.
327. *Theol. Gr. Patr.*, book 2, c. 6.
328. Ibid., c. 15.

some sort efficacious" (*secundum quid*) because of its effect commenced but not completed. Lastly, he says that sufficient grace is the grace of prayer, of which it is in our power to avail ourselves, as St. Augustine teaches. So that a man has no excuse if he does not do that which he already has sufficient grace to enable him to perform; by which grace, without further assistance, he may either act, or at least obtain more help to enable him to act. And Habert asserts that this was the common doctrine of the Sorbonne.

Charles du Plessis d'Argentré, another theologian of the Sorbonne, quotes more than a thousand theologians who teach directly that with sufficient grace easy works are accomplished; and that a man who makes use of it obtains thereby a more abundant assistance for his thorough conversion. And precisely in this sense, as we said before, he says the celebrated axiom of the schools is to be understood: "To those who do what is in their power [that is, by means of sufficient grace], God does not deny grace"[329]—that is, more abundant and efficacious grace.

The learned Dionysius Petavius proves at great length that man works with simple sufficient grace; and he even asserts that it would be monstrous to say otherwise; and that this is the doctrine not only of theologians, but also of the Church. Hence he says that the grace of observing the precepts follows prayer; and that the gift of prayer is given by God at the time when he imposes the precept: "This gift, by which God grants us power to do justly, follows the act of prayer; and this act is given contemporaneously with the law." So that as the law is imposed upon all, so the gift of prayer is given to all.

The author of the *Theology for the Use of the Seminary of Peterkau* says that with sufficient grace alone "a man can do well, and sometimes does so," so that "there is nothing to hinder that, of two persons furnished with the same assistance, one should very often perform the mere acts [which precede full conversion], the other not."[330] And this, he says, is in conformity with the doctrine of St. Augustine and St. Thomas, and of his first disciples, especially of Father Bartholomew Medina, who says, "Sometimes a man is converted only with sufficient grace."[331] And I find

329. *De Deo*, book 10, c. 20, 19.
330. Book 6, q. 3.
331. *In* 1.2, q. 109, a. 10.

that also Father Louis of Granada asserts this to be the common doctrine of theologians: "Theologians reckon two kinds of assistance, one sufficient, the other more than sufficient; by the former of which men are sometimes converted, sometimes refuse to be converted." And, shortly afterward, "And theologians define how universally this assistance is open to men."[332] Hence Petrocorensis says, "So man can do some acts of piety, such as to pray to God with humility with the sufficient grace only, and sometimes actually does them, and so prepares himself for further graces." This, he says, is the order of God's Providence with regard to graces, "that the succeeding should follow the good use of the former."[333] And he concludes that thorough conversion and final perseverance "are infallibly obtained by prayer, for which the sufficient grace which is given to everyone abundantly suffices."

The same is held by Cardinal d'Aguirre, who in all things follows St. Augustine.[334]

Father Antonio Boucat, of the order of St. Francis of Paula, defends the position that everyone is now able, without new assistance, to obtain by prayer the grace of conversion. And after quoting Gamaches, Duval, Habert, and Le Moyne, he cites in favor of this opinion Peter of Tarantasia, Bishop of Tulle, Godert de Fonte, and Henry of Ghent, Doctors of the Sorbonne, together with the Regius Professor Lygne, who, in his tract *De Gratia*, demonstrates that "sufficient grace" not only gives prayer, as Le Moyne and Professor Elias said, but also gives the power to do some works that are not difficult.

Gaudenzio Bontempi in like manner demonstrated that sufficient grace obtains efficacious grace by means of prayer, which is given to all who will avail themselves of it.

Cardinal Robert Pullo asserts two kinds of grace, one always victorious, the other one by which man sometimes works, sometimes does not: "The other by the asistance of which man can do which he chooses of these two things, either to cooperate with grace, or to despise it and to continue sinning."[335]

---

332. *In fest. S. Matt. conc.* 1, p. 1.

333. *Loco sup. cit.*

334. *Theol. S. Ans.*, vol. 3, d. 125, 126, 127.

335. *Sent.*, book 6, c. 50.

Father Fortunate da Brescia is also of the same opinion, and holds that all men have the mediate grace of prayer to enable them to observe the precepts and has no doubt that St. Augustine held the same.

Richard of St. Victor similarly teaches that there is a sufficient grace which a man sometimes consents to, sometimes resists.

Dominic Soto asks, "Why of two persons whom God is most ready and desirous to convert, one is drawn by grace, and not the other?" And he answers, "No other reason can be given, except that one consents and cooperates, while the other does not cooperate."[336]

Matthias Felicio, who wrote against Calvin, thus defines ordinary or sufficient grace: "It is a divine motion, or instinct, which moves a man to good and is denied to none. Men behave differently to this instinct; for some acquiesce in it, and are disposed *de congruo* for habitual grace; for we believe that God will not desert those who do what they can. Others, on the contrary, oppose it."[337]

Andreas Vega likewise says: "These helps, which are given to all men, are by most called inefficacious because they do not always produce their effect but are sometimes frustrated by sinners."[338] Therefore, sufficient grace sometimes produces its effect and sometimes does not.

Cardinal Gotti in one place of his *Theology* apparently agrees with us; for where he discusses the difficulty, how a man can persevere if he will when it is not in his power to have the special assistance which is requisite for perseverance, he answers that although this special assistance is not in a man's power, "yet it is said to be in a man's power, because he can by the grace of God ask for it and obtain it; and in this way it may be said to be in a man's power to have the assistance necessary for perseverance, because it can be obtained by prayers."[339] So to verify the proposition that it is in a man's power to persevere, it is necessary to grant both that he can, without needing any further grace, obtain by prayer the assistance requisite for perseverance, and also that with only the sufficient grace common to all, without need of any special grace, he can actually pray, and by prayer obtain perseverance; otherwise it could not be said that

---

336. *De Nat. et Gr.*, book 1, c. 15.
337. *Inst. Chr.*, d. 24, c. 20.
338. *De Justif.*, book 13, c. 13.
339. *De Grat.* q. 1, d. 13, s. 3.

every man had the grace necessary for perseverance, at least remotely or mediately, by means of prayer.

But if Cardinal Gotti did not mean this, at any rate St. Francis de Sales did when he said that the grace of actual prayer is given to everyone who will avail himself of it, and thence deduced that perseverance is in the power of everybody. The saint says this clearly in his *Theotimus*, where, after proving that constant prayer is necessary to obtain from God the gift of final perseverance, he adds, "Now, since the gift of prayer is freely promised to all those who will consent to the heavenly inspirations, consequently it is in our power to persevere."

Cardinal Bellarmine teaches the same thing: "An assistance, then and there, sufficient for salvation, is given mediately or immediately to all men. . . . We say mediately or immediately because to those who have the use of reason we believe that holy inspirations are given by God, and that by this they have immediately the exciting grace; by which, if they will acquiesce in it, they can be disposed to be justified, and at last to obtain salvation."[340]

II.   Authority upon which this doctrine is based

Let us now proceed to examine the proofs of this doctrine. It is proved, first from authority. We shall cite Scripture, the Council of Trent, and the Holy Fathers.

1. HOLY SCRIPTURE

We have first the authority of the Apostle, who assures us that God is faithful and will not permit us to be tempted beyond our strength, since he always gives us assistance (whether immediate or mediate, by means of prayer) to resist the assaults of our enemies: "God is faithful, who will not suffer you to be tempted above that you are able, but will make with the temptation issue, that you may be able to bear it" (1 Corinthians 10:13). Jansen says that this text refers only to the predestinate, but this comment of his is completely unfounded; for St. Paul is writing to all the faithful of Corinth, all of whom he certainly did not consider to be

---

340.   *De Gr. et Lib. Arb.*, book 2, c. 5.

predestinate. So that St. Thomas has good reason for understanding it generally of all men, and for saying that God would not be faithful if he did not grant us (so far as in him lies) those graces by means of which we can obtain salvation: "But he would not appear to be faithful were he to refuse us [so far as he is concerned] those things which are requisite to enable us to come to him."[341] It is proved, moreover, by all those texts in which God exhorts us to convert ourselves, and to have recourse to him to ask him for the graces necessary for our salvation, and promises to hear us when we have recourse to him. "Wisdom preaches aloud . . . saying, O children, how long will you love childishness, and fools covet those things which are hurtful to themselves, etc.? Turn at my reproof: behold, I will utter my Spirit to you. . . . Because I called, and you refused, etc., I also will laugh in your destruction, and will mock at you" (Proverbs 1:20–23). This exhortation, "Turn you," would be simple mockery, says Bellarmine, if God did not give to sinners at least the mediate grace of prayer for their conversion. Besides, we find in the passage mention made of the internal grace by which God calls sinners and gives them actual assistance for conversion, if they will accept it, in the words, "Behold, I will bring forth my Spirit to you." "Come to me, all you that labor and are heavy laden, and I will refresh you" (Matthew 11:28). "Come, and accuse me, says the Lord; if your sins are as scarlet, they shall be made white as snow" (Isaiah 1:18). "Ask, and it shall be given you" (Matthew 7:7). And so in hundreds of other texts already quoted. Now, if God did not give everyone grace actually to have recourse to him, and actually to pray to him, all these invitations and exhortations, "Come all, and I will refresh you," "Seek, and it shall be given you," would be vain.

2. THE COUNCIL OF TRENT

It is clearly proved by the passage of the Council of Trent so often quoted.[342] I beg the reader to give his best attention to this proof, which, if I am not mistaken, is perfectly decisive. There were innovators who said that as man was deprived of free-will by the sin of Adam, the will of man at present does nothing in good actions but is induced to receive

---

341. *In 1 Cor. 1*, lect. 1.
342. Sess. 6, c. 4.

them passively from God, without producing them itself; and hence they inferred that the observance of the commandments was impossible to those who are not efficaciously moved and predetermined by grace to avoid evil and to do good. Against this error the Council pronounced sentence in words borrowed from St. Augustine: "God does not command impossible things; but by commanding, admonishes you both to do what you can and to pray for what you cannot do; and he helps you, so that you may be able."

The Council, then, in order to prove against the heretics that God's commandments are not impossible to anyone, has declared that all men have assistance to enable them to do good, or at least have the grace of prayer whereby to obtain greater assistance. The meaning of this is that every man can, by means of the common grace, do easy things (such as pray) without need of further extraordinary grace and can by prayer obtain strength to do difficult things, according to the teaching of St. Augustine, already quoted: "By the very fact that we most firmly believe that the good and just God could not have commanded impossible things, we are admonished in easy matters what to do and in difficult matters what to pray for."[343] So that, according to the Council, the divine precepts are possible to all men, at least by means of prayer, by which greater help may be obtained to enable us to observe them. If, therefore, God has imposed his commands on all men and has rendered their observance possible to all, at least mediately by means of prayer, we must necessarily conclude that all men have the grace to enable them to pray; otherwise, the commandments would not be possible to him who was without this grace. And as God grants to prayer actual grace to do good, and thereby renders all his commandments possible, so also he gives all actual grace to pray; otherwise, if there were any man who had not actual grace to pray to him, the commandments would be impossible, as he could not even by means of prayer obtain the assistance necessary for their observance.

This being settled, it is of no use to say that the words "God admonishes you to do what you can, and to ask for what you cannot do" are only to be understood of possible, not of actual, prayer, because, we reply, if the common and ordinary grace gave only possible and not actual prayer,

---

343. *De Nat. et Grat.*, c. 69.

the Council would not have said, "He admonishes you to do what you can, and to ask for what you cannot do," but, "He admonishes you that you can do, and that you can pray." Moreover, if the Council had not intended to declare that everyone can observe the precepts, or can pray to obtain grace to observe them, and had not meant to speak of actual grace, it would not have said, "He admonishes," because this word properly refers to actual operation and imports not the instruction of the mind, but the movement of the will to do that good which it can actually do. When, therefore, it said, "He admonishes you to do what you can, and to ask for what you cannot do," it most clearly expressed not only possible operation and possible prayer, but actual operation and actual prayer. For if man had need of another extraordinary grace, which as yet he has not, in order actually to work or to pray, how could God admonish him to do or to ask that which he cannot actually either do or ask without efficacious grace? Father Fortunate Brescia speaks wisely on this point: If the actual grace of prayer were not given to all, but if for prayer we had need of efficacious grace, which is not common to all, prayer would be impossible to the great number who are without this efficacious grace, so that it could not be said with propriety that "God admonishes you to ask for that which you cannot do," because he would then admonish us to do a thing requiring a grace which we did not possess. So that God's admonition to work and to pray must be understood of actual operation and prayer, without need of a further extraordinary grace. And this is exactly what St. Augustine means: "Hence we are admonished in easy things what to do, and in difficult things what to pray for," because he supposes that though all do not have grace to enable them to do difficult things, all have at least grace to pray—prayer being an easy thing for everybody—as he also propounds in the words afterward adopted by the Council of Trent, "God admonishes you to do what you can, and to ask for what you cannot do."

To recapitulate the argument: The Council says that God does not impose impossible commands, because he either gives assistance to observe them or gives the grace of prayer to obtain this assistance, which he always grants when it is prayed for. Now, if it could ever be true that God does not give all men grace, at least the mediate grace of prayer, actually to observe all his precepts, Jansen's proposition would be true, that even the just man is without grace to enable him actually to observe some of the commandments.

I do not know how else the text of the Council of Trent can be understood and explained, unless the "sufficient grace" gave to all men the power of actually praying without the "efficacious grace" which our opponents suppose to be necessary for the actual performance of any pious work. And supposing this necessity of a further grace for actual prayer, I cannot understand how this other text of the same Council can be true: "God does not leave those who have been once justified without grace, unless they first leave him."[344] If, I say, the ordinary sufficient grace would not be enough for actual prayer, but if for this purpose efficacious grace, which is not common to all men, would be required, it would be true that when the just man would be tempted to commit his first mortal sin, and God would not give him efficacious grace at least to enable him to pray and so to obtain strength to resist, then his succumbing to temptation might rather be said to result from the just man being abandoned by God before he had abandoned God, and from being left without the efficacious grace necessary to enable him to resist.

Our opponents object to us a passage of St. Augustine where he appears to maintain that the grace of prayer is not granted to all men: "Is not our prayer itself at times so tepid, or rather so cold, and almost null—so null, indeed, that we do not notice its nullity with any sorrow; for if this coldness is against our will, it does not prejudice our prayer?"[345] But Cardinal Sfondrati well replies, "It is one thing to say that sinners do not pray, another to say that they have not grace to enable them to pray."[346] St. Augustine does not say that any persons are without grace to pray as they ought, but only that at times our prayer is so cold as to be almost null, not for want of God's assistance to enable us to pray better, but simply through our fault, which renders our prayer null. Tourneley answers in the same way where he says of the first condemned proposition of Jansen: "The just do not always pray as they ought. It is their own fault that they do not pray so, since they have by grace sufficient

344. Sess. 6, c. 11.
345. *Ad Simpl.*, book 1, q. 2.
346. *Nod. praed.*, p. 1, s. 2.

strength to pray. St. Augustine says that our prayer is sometimes cold and almost null; but he does not say that we have not grace to enable us to pray more fervently."[347] Moreover, Cardinal Noris observes on this same passage that by means of tepid prayer we can at least obtain grace to pray more fervently, and then by this we obtain efficacious grace to keep the commandments: "I conclude that even tepid prayer is made with the assistance *sine quo non*, and by the ordinary help of God, since they are weak acts, etc. .... And yet by tepid prayer we obtain the spirit of more fervent prayer, which is given to us by the assistance *quo*."[348] And he confirms this by the authority of St. Augustine, who writes thus on Psalm 17: "I have directed my prayers unto you with a free and strong intention; for you did hear me when I prayed more weakly, and did grant me strength for this."[349]

Nor can a valid objection be drawn from St. Augustine's observation on the text of St. Paul, "The Spirit beseeches for us with groans not to be uttered" (Romans 8:26), that it is the Holy Spirit that makes us intercede, and inspires us with the disposition to intercede,[350] since the saint here simply says, against the Pelagians, that no one can pray without grace. And thus he himself explains it in his commentary on Psalm 53, where he says, "What you do by his gift, he is said to do; because without him you could not do it."[351]

3. THE HOLY FATHERS

In the third place, our opinion is proved by the sayings of the holy Fathers.

St. Basil says: "When, however, anyone is allowed to fall into temptation, it happens that he may be able to endure it, and to ask in prayer that the will of God may be done."[352] The saint then says that when God permits a man to be tempted, he does it in order that the man may resist by asking for God's will, i.e., the grace to overcome. He therefore supposes

---

347. *De Gr. Chr.*, q. 3, p. 1.
348. *Jans. err. cal. subl.*, c. 3.
349. Psalm 16 in the Vulgate. *In Ps. xvi.*
350. *Ep.* 194, c. 4, E. B.
351. Psalm 52 in the Vulgate. *In Ps. lii.*
352. *Mor. reg.* 62, c. 2.

that when a man has not sufficient assistance to overcome the temptation, he at least has the actual and common grace of prayer, by which he may obtain whatever further grace he needs.

St. John Chrysostom says, "He gave a law which might make their wounds manifest, in order that they might desire a physician."[353] And again: "Nor can anyone be excused who, by ceasing to pray, has voluntarily abstained from overcoming his adversary.[354] If such a man had not the grace necessary for actual prayer, whereby he might obtain grace to resist, he might excuse himself when he is overcome.

So also St. Bernard: "Who are we, or what is our strength? This is what God wanted: that we, seeing our weakness and that we have no other help, should with all humility have recourse to his mercy."[355] God, then, has imposed on us a law impossible to our own strength, in order that we should go to him and, by prayer, obtain strength to observe it; but if anyone were without the grace of actual prayer, to him the Law would be utterly impossible. "Many persons," says the same St. Bernard, "complain that they are deserted by grace; but grace could much more justly complain of being deserted by them."[356] God has much more reason to complain of us for not corresponding to the grace he gives us than we have to complain of not having grace to which we may correspond.

But no Father is more clear on this point than St. Augustine in several places. In one he says: "The Pelagians think themselves very knowing when they say, 'God would not command that which he knows man could not do. Who is ignorant of this?' But God does command some things that we cannot do, in order that we might know that for which we ought to ask him."[357]

Again, "It is not reckoned your fault if you are ignorant without wishing to be so, but only if you neglect to inquire into that of which you are ignorant; nor that you do not cure your wounded members, but that you despise him who is willing to heal you. These are your own sins; for no

353. *In Gall.* 3:22.
354. *Hom. de Moys.*
355. *In Quad.*, s. 5.
356. *De Div.*, s. 17.
357. *De Gr. et Lib. Arb..* c. 16.

man is deprived of the knowledge of how to seek with advantage."[358] So that, according to St. Augustine, no one is deprived of the grace of prayer, whereby he may obtain help for his conversion; otherwise, if this grace were wanting, it could not be his fault if he were not converted.

Again: "What else, then, is shown us, but that it is God who gives us power both to ask, and to seek, and to knock, who commands us to do these things?"[359]

Again: "Once for all, receive this and understand it. Are you not yet drawn? Pray that you may be drawn."[360]

Again: "That the soul, then, knows not what it ought to do comes from this: that it has not yet received it, but it will receive this also if it has made a good use of what it has received; and it has received power to seek piously and diligently if it will."[361] Mark the words "it has received power to seek diligently and piously." Everyone, then, has the grace necessary for prayer; and if he makes a good use of this, he will receive grace to do that which before he was unable to do immediately.

Again: "Let the man who is willing, but cannot do what he wills, pray that he may have such a measure as suffices for fulfilling the commandments; for he is so far assisted as to be able to do what is commanded."[362] Again: "Freewill is admonished by command to seek the gift of God; but it would be admonished without fruit to itself unless it had first received some little love, to induce it to seek such aid as would enable it to fulfill what was commanded."[363] Mark the words "some little love"—this means "sufficient grace" whereby man is able to obtain by prayer actual grace to keep the commandments, whereby "he is induced to seek such aid as would enable him to fulfill what was commanded."

Again: "He gives us commandments for this reason: that when we have tried to do what we are commanded and are wearied through our infirmity, we may know how to ask the help of grace."[364] Here the saint

---

358. *De Lib. Arb.*, book 3, c. 19.
359. *Ad Simpl.*, book 1, q. 2.
360. *In Jo.*, tr. 26.
361. *De Lib. Arb.*, book 3, c. 22.
362. *De Gr. et Lib. Arb.*, c. 15.
363. *De Gr. et Lib. Arb.*, c. 18.
364. Ep. 157, E. B.

supposes that with ordinary grace we are not able to do difficult things, but can by means of prayer obtain the aid necessary to accomplish them. Hence he goes on to say, "The Law entered that sin might abound" (Romans 5:20) when men do not implore the aid of God's grace; but when, by God's vocation, they understand to whom they must groan and thereupon invoke him, the succeeding words will be fulfilled: "Where sin abounded, grace superabounded." Here, as Petavius says, we see in express terms the want of abundant grace; and, on the other hand, the presence of ordinary and common grace which enables men to pray, and which St. Augustine here calls "God's vocation."

In another place he says, "Freewill is left to man in this mortal life not to enable him to fulfill justice when he pleases, but to enable him to turn with pious supplications to him by whose gift he can fulfill it."[365] When, therefore, Augustine says that man is unable to fulfill the whole law, and that prayer is the only means given him to obtain help to fulfill it, he certainly supposes that God gives every man the grace of actual prayer, without need of a further extraordinary aid not common to all men; otherwise, where this special aid was wanting, "nothing would be left to the will" to observe all the commandments, or at least the more difficult of them. And when the saint speaks thus, he certainly cannot mean that "sufficient grace" gives only the power, not the act of prayer; for so far as relates to power, it is certain that "sufficient grace" gives power for even the most difficult works. Hence the holy Father evidently means (as he teaches elsewhere) that easy things, such as prayer, may well be actually accomplished by any man with the "sufficient grace," and difficult things with the help which is obtained by means of prayer.

But there are two texts of St. Augustine which are peculiarly to the point.

The first is this: "It is certain that we can keep the commandments if we will; but since the will is prepared by God, we must ask him that we may have such a will as is sufficient to enable us to perform what we will."[366] Here he says that it is certain we could observe the law if we would; on the other hand, he says that in order to will to do so, and actually to do

---

365. *Ad Simpl.*, book 1, q. 1.
366. *De Gr. et Lib. Arb.*, c. 16.

so, we must pray. Therefore all men have grace given them to pray and, by prayer, to obtain the abundant grace which makes us keep the commandments; otherwise, if for actual prayer, efficacious grace, which is not common to all, were requisite, those to whom it was not given would not be able to keep the commandments nor to have the will to keep them.

The second text is that where the holy Doctor answers the monks of Adramyttium, who said: "If grace was necessary, and if we can do nothing without it, why blame when we cannot work and have not grace to do so? You should rather pray God for us that he would give us this grace." St. Augustine answers, you must be blamed not because you do not work when you have not strength, but because you do not pray to obtain strength: "He who will not be admonished and says, 'You, rather, pray for me,' must on that very account be admonished to do it [i.e., to pray] for himself."[367] Now if the saint had not believed that every man has grace, to pray (if he will) without need of further aid, he never could have said that these people were to be blamed for not praying; for they could have answered that if they were not to be blamed for not working, when they had not special grace to enable them to work; in like manner they could not be blamed for not praying, when they had not special grace for actual prayer. This is what St. Augustine elsewhere says: "Let them not deceive themselves who say, 'Why are we commanded to abstain from evil and do good if it is God who works in us both to will and to do it?'"[368] And he answers that when men do good they should thank God for it, who gives them strength to do it; and when they do it not, they should pray to have the strength which they lack: "But when they do it not"—these are his words—"let them pray that they may receive that which as yet they have not." Now if these people had not even the grace for the act of prayer, they might answer, "Why are we commanded to pray, if God does not work in us to make us pray? How are we to will to pray, if we do not receive the grace necessary for actual prayer?"

St. Thomas does not speak expressly of prayer but assumes the certainty of our proposition when he says, "It belongs to God's Providence to provide every individual with what is necessary for salvation, provided

---

367. *De Corr. et Gr.*, c. 5.
368. *De Corr. et Gr.*, c. 2.

he puts no impediment in the way."[369] Since, then, it is true, on the one hand that God gives to all men the graces necessary for salvation, and on the other, for prayer we require the grace which enables us actually to pray, and thereby to obtain further and greater assistance to enable us to do that which we cannot compass with ordinary grace, it follows necessarily that God gives all men sufficient grace actually to pray if they will, without need of efficacious grace.

Here we may add the answer of Bellarmine to the heretics, who inferred from the text, "No one can come to me, unless my Father draws him" (John 6:44), that no one could go to God who was not properly drawn by him. "We answer," he says, "that the only conclusion from this text is that all men have not the efficacious grace to make them really believe; but we cannot conclude that all men have not at least assistance which confers the possibility of believing, or, at any rate, the possibility of asking for grace."[370]

III. Reasons that justify this doctrine

Let us now proceed, in the third and last place, to examine the reasons of this opinion. Petavius, Duval, and other theologians ask why God imposes on us commands which we cannot keep with the common and ordinary grace. Because, they answer, he wishes us to have recourse to him in prayer, according to the general consent of the Fathers, as we have seen above. Hence they infer that we ought to hold it to be certain that every man has grace actually to pray, and by prayer to obtain greater grace to enable him to do that which is impossible to him with the ordinary grace; otherwise God would have imposed an impossible law.

This reason is very strong. Another is that if God imposes on all men the duty of actual observance of his commandments, we must necessarily suppose that he also gives to all men the grace necessary for this actual observance, at least mediately, by means of prayer. In order, therefore, to uphold the reasonableness of the law and the justice of the punishment of the disobedient, we must hold that every man has sufficient power, at

---

369. *De Verit.*, q. 14, a. 11.
370. *De Gr. et Lib. Arb.*, book 2, c. 8.

least mediately, by means of prayer, for the actual satisfaction of the law; and that at times he prays without need of an unusual and additional grace; otherwise, if he had not this mediate or remote power of actually keeping the commandments, it could never be said that all men had from God sufficient grace for the actual observance of the law.

Thomassin and Tourneley accumulate many other reasons for this opinion; but I pass them over to attend to one that seems to me demonstrative. It is founded on the precept of hope, which obliges us all to hope in God with confidence for eternal life; and I say that if we were not certain that God gives us all grace to enable us actually to pray, without need of another particular and unusual grace, no one without a special revelation could hope for salvation as he ought. But I must first explain the grounds of this argument.

The virtue of hope is so pleasing to God that he has declared that he feels delight in those who trust in him: "The Lord takes pleasure in them that hope in his mercy" (Psalm 147:11). And he promises victory over his enemies, perseverance in grace, and eternal glory, to the man who hopes, because he hopes: "Because he hoped in me, I will deliver him; I will protect him. . . . I will deliver him and I will glorify him" (Psalm 91:14). "Preserve me, for I have put my trust in you" (Psalm 37:40). "He will save them because they have hoped in him" (Psalm 16:1). "No one has hoped in the Lord and has been confounded" (Sirach 2:10). And let us be sure that the heaven and earth will fail, but the promises of God cannot fail: "Heaven and earth shall pass away, but my words shall not pass away" (Matthew 24:35). St. Bernard, therefore, says that all our merit consists in reposing all our confidence in God: "This is the whole merit of man, if he places all his hope in him."[371] The reason is that he who hopes in God honors him much: "Call upon me in the day of trouble; I will deliver you, and you shall glorify me" (Psalm 50:15). He honors the power, the mercy, and the faithfulness of God, since he believes that God can and will save him, and that he cannot fail in his promises to save the man who trusts in him. And the Prophet assures us that the greater is our confidence, the greater will be the measure of God's mercy poured out upon us: "Let your mercy, O Lord, be upon us, as we have hoped in you" (Psalm 33:22).

---

371. *In Ps. xc.*, s. 15.

Now, as this virtue of hope is so pleasing to God, he has willed to impose it upon us by a precept that binds under mortal sin, as all theologians agree, and as is evident from many texts of Scripture. "Trust in him, all you congregations of people" (Psalm 62:9). "You that fear the Lord, hope in him" (Sirach 2:9). "Hope in your God always" (Hosea 12:7). "Hope perfectly for that grace which is offered to you" (1 Peter 1:13). Then this hope of eternal life ought to be sure and firm in us, according to the definition of St. Thomas: "Hope is the certain expectation of beatitude."[372] And the sacred Council of Trent has expressly declared, "All men ought to place and repose a most firm hope in the help of God; for God, unless they fail to correspond to his grace, as he has begun the good work, so will he finish it, working in them both to will and to perform."[373] And long before St. Paul had said of himself: "I know whom I have believed, and I am certain that he is able to keep what I have committed to him" (1 Timothy 1:12). And herein is the difference between Christian and worldly hope. Worldly hope need only be an uncertain expectation: nor can it be otherwise, for it is always doubtful whether a man who has promised a favor may not hereafter change his mind, if he has not already changed it. But the Christian hope of eternal salvation is certain on God's part; for he can and will save us, and has promised to save those who obey his law, and to this end has promised us all necessary graces to enable us to obey this law if we ask for them. It is true that hope is accompanied by fear, as St. Thomas says; but this fear does not arise from God's part, but from our own, since we may at any time fail, by not corresponding as we ought and by putting an impediment in the way of grace by our sins. Reasonably, then, did the Council of Trent condemn the innovators, who, because they entirely deprive man of free will, are obliged to make every believer have an infallible certitude of perseverance and salvation. This error was condemned by the Council because, as we have said, in order to obtain salvation, it is necessary for us to correspond; and this correspondence of ours is uncertain and fallible. Hence God wills that we should, on the one hand, always fear for ourselves, lest we should fall into presumption in trusting to our strength; but, on the other that we

---

372. *Summa*, 2.2, q. 18, a. 4.
373. Sess. 6, c. 13.

should be always certain of his good will, and of his assistance to save us, provided always that we ask him for it; in other words, that we might always have a secure confidence in his goodness. St. Thomas says that we ought to look with certainty to receive from God eternal happiness, confiding in his power and mercy, and believing that he can and will save us. "Whoever has faith is certain of God's power and mercy."

Now, as the hope of our salvation by God ought to be certain, (as St. Thomas defines it) "the certain expectation of beatitude," consequently the motive of our hope must also be certain; for if the foundation of our hope were uncertain and admitted a doubt, we could not with any certainty hope and expect to receive salvation and the means necessary for it from the hands of God. But St. Paul will have us to be nothing less than firm and immovable in our hope if we would be saved: "If so you continue in the faith, grounded and settled and immovable from the hope of the Gospel which you have heard" (Colossians 1:23). In another place he repeats that our faith ought to be as immovable as an anchor securely fixed; since it is grounded on the promises of God, who cannot lie: "And we desire that every one of you should show forth the same carefulness to the accomplishing of hope unto the end. . . . That by two immutable things, in which it is impossible for God to lie, we may have the strongest comfort, who have fled for refuge to hold fast the hope set before us, which we have as an anchor of the soul, sure and firm" (Hebrews 6:11–19). Hence St. Bernard says that our hope cannot be uncertain, as it rests on God's promises: "Nor does this expectation seem to us vain, or this hope doubtful, since we rely on the promises of the eternal truth."[374] In another place he says of himself that his hope depends on three things: the love which induced God to adopt us as his children, the truth of his promises, and his power to fulfill them. "Three things I see in which my hope consists: the love of adoption, the truth of promise, the power of performance."[375]

And therefore the Apostle St. James declares that the man who desires the grace of God must ask for it, not with hesitation, but with the confident certainty of obtaining it: "Let him ask in faith, nothing wavering."

---

374. *In Ps. xc.*, s. 7.
375. *Dom. 6 p. Pent.*, s. 3.

For if he asks with hesitation, he shall obtain nothing: "For he who wavers is like a wave of the sea that is moved and carried about by the wind; therefore, let not that man think that he shall receive anything of the Lord" (James 1:6). And St. Paul praises Abraham for not doubting God's promise, as he knew that when God promises, he cannot fail to perform: "In the promise, also, of God, he staggered not by distrust but was strengthened in faith, giving glory to God, most fully knowing that whatsoever he has promised, he is able also to perform" (Romans 4:20). Hence, also, Jesus Christ tells us that we shall then receive all the graces that we desire when we ask them with a sure belief of receiving them: "Therefore I say to you, all things whatsoever you ask when you pray, believe that you shall receive them, and they shall come unto you." In a word, God will not hear us unless we have a sure confidence of being heard.

Now let us come to the point. Our hope of salvation and of receiving the means necessary for its attainment must be certain on God's part. The motives on which this certainty are founded, as we have seen, are the power, the mercy, and the truth of God; and of these the strongest and most certain motive is God's infallible faithfulness to the promise which he has made to us, through the merits of Jesus Christ, to save us and to give us the graces necessary for our salvation, because though we might believe God to be infinite in power and mercy, nevertheless, as Giovenino well observes, we could not feel confident expectation of God's saving us unless he had surely promised to do so. But this promise is conditional—if we actively correspond to God's grace and pray, as is clear from the Scriptures: "Ask, and you shall receive"; "If you ask the Father anything in my name, he will give it you"; "He will give good things to those who ask him"; "We ought always to pray"; "You have not, because you ask not"; "If anyone wants wisdom, let him ask of God"; and many other texts which we have quoted before. For this cause the Fathers and theologians, as we showed in part I, chapter I, maintain that prayer is a necessary means of salvation.

Now, if we were not certain that God gives to all men grace to enable them actually to pray, without need of a further, special, and unusual grace, we could have no certain and firm foundation for a certain hope of salvation in God, but only an uncertain and conditional foundation. When I am certain that by prayer I shall obtain eternal life and all the graces necessary to attain it; and when I know that God will not deny me the grace of actual prayer, if I will (because he gives it to all men); then I have a sure foundation for hoping in God for salvation, unless I fail on my part. But when I am in doubt whether or not God will give me that particular grace which he does not give to all, but which is necessary for actual prayer, then I have not a certain foundation for my hope of salvation, but only a doubtful and uncertain one, since I cannot be sure that God will give me this special grace without which I cannot pray, since he refuses it to so many. And in this case the uncertainty would not be only on my part, but also on God's part; and so Christian hope would be destroyed, which, according to the Apostle, ought to be immovable, firm, and secure. I really cannot see how a Christian can fulfill the precept of hope—hoping, as he ought, with sure confidence for salvation from God and for the graces necessary for its attainment—unless he holds it as an infallible truth that God commonly gives to every individual the grace actually to pray, if he chooses, without need of a further special assistance.

So that, to conclude, our system or opinion (held by so many theologians and by our humble Congregation) well agrees, on the one hand, with the doctrine of grace intrinsically efficacious, by means of which we infallibly, though freely, act virtuously.

It cannot be denied that God can easily, with his omnipotence, incline and move men's hearts freely to will that which he wills, as the Scriptures teach: "The heart of the king is in the hand of the Lord; whithersoever he will, he shall turn it" (Proverbs 21:1). "I will put my Spirit in the midst of you, and I will cause you to walk in my commandments" (Ezekiel 36:27). "My counsel shall stand, and all my will shall be done" (Isaiah 46:10). "He changes the heart of the princes of the people of the earth" (Job 12:24). "May the God of peace make you perfect in every good work, that you may do his will, working in you that which is well-pleasing in his sight, through Jesus Christ" (Hebrews 13:21).

And it cannot be denied that St. Augustine and St. Thomas have taught the opinion of the efficaciousness of grace in itself, by its own nature. This is evident from many passages, and specially from the following:

St. Augustine says: "Yet God did not this, except by the will of the men themselves; since he, no doubt, has the most almighty and absolute power of inclining the hearts of men."[376] Again: "Almighty God works in the hearts of men, that he may do by their means that which he has determined to do."[377] Again: "Although they all do what is right in the service of God, yet he causes them to do what he commands."[378] Again: "It is certain that we act when we act; but he causes us to act by bestowing most efficacious powers on the will, according to his words, 'I will make you to walk in my justifications'" (Ezekiel 36:27).[379] Again, on the text, "For it is God that works in you, both to will and accomplish according to his good will" (Philippians 2:13), he says, "We therefore will; but God works in us, both to will and to perform."[380] Again: "As the will is prepared by God, we must pray that we may have as much will as is sufficient to make us act when we will."[381] Again: "God knows how to work in men's hearts, not so as to make them believe against their will, which is impossible, but so as to make them willing instead of unwilling."[382] Again: "He works in men's hearts, not only true revelations, but also goodwill."[383] Again: "Our acts of will have just so much power as God chooses them to have."[384] Again: "The wills which preserve the system of creation are in such sort in God's power, that he makes them incline where he will and when he will."[385] So St. Thomas: "God infallibly moves the will by the efficacy of the moving power, which cannot fail."[386] Again: "Love has the character of impeccability, from the power of the Holy Spirit, who infallibly works whatever he will; hence it is impossible that these two things should be at the same time true: that the Holy Spirit wills to move a person to an act of love, and that at the same time the person should

---

376. *De Cor. et Gr.*, c. 14.
377. *De Gr. et Lib. Arb.*, c. 21.
378. *De Praed. SS.*, c. 10.
379. *De Gr. et Lib. Arb.*, c. 16.
380. *De Dono. Pers.*, c. 13.
381. *De Gr. et Lib. Arb.*, c. 16.
382. *Ad Bonif.*, book 1, c. 19.
383. *De Gr. Chr.*, c. 24.
384. *De Civ. D.*, book 5, c. 9.
385. *De Gr. et Lib. Arb.*, c. 20.
386. *De Mal.*, q. 6, ad 3.

lose love by an act of sin."[387] Again: "If God moves the will to anything, it is impossible to say that the will is not moved to it."[388]

On the other hand, our opinion is quite consonant to the doctrine of truly sufficient grace being given to all, by corresponding to which a man will gain efficacious grace; while by not corresponding, but resisting, he will deservedly be refused this efficacious grace. And thus all excuse is taken away from those sinners who say that they have not strength to overcome their temptations; because if they had prayed and made use of the ordinary grace which is given to all men, they would have obtained strength and would have been saved. Otherwise, if a person does not admit this ordinary grace by which everyone is enabled at least to pray (without needing a further special and unusual grace), and by prayer to obtain further assistance to enable him to fulfill the law, I do not know how he can explain all those texts of the Scripture in which souls are exhorted to return to God, to overcome temptation, and to correspond to the divine call: "Return, you transgressors, to the heart" (Isaiah 46:8); "Return and live; be converted, and do penance" (Ezekiel 18:30, 32); "Loose the bonds from off your neck" (Isaiah 52:2); "Come to me, all you that labor and are burdened" (Matthew 11:28); "Resist, strong in faith" (1 Peter 5:9); "Walk while you have the light" (John 12:35). I cannot tell, I say, supposing it were true that the grace of prayer were not given to all to enable them thereby to obtain the further assistance necessary for salvation, how these texts could be explained, and how the sacred writers could so forcibly exhort all men, without any exception, to be converted, to resist the enemy, to walk in the way of virtue, and, for this end, to pray with confidence and perseverance if the grace of doing well, or at least of praying, were not granted to all, but only to those who have the gift of efficacious grace. And I cannot see where would be the justice of the reproof given to all sinners without exception, who resist grace and despise the voice of God: "You always resist the Holy Spirit" (Acts 7:51); "Because I called and you refused; I stretched out my hand, and there was none that regarded; you have despised all my counsel, and have neglected my reprehensions" (Proverbs 1:24–25). If they were without

---

387. *Summa*, 2.2, q. 24, a. 11.
388. *Summa*, 1.2, q. 10, a. 4.

even the remote but efficacious grace of prayer, which our opponents consider necessary for actual prayer, I cannot tell how all these reproofs could be justly made against them.

Conclusion

I have done. Some, perhaps, will wish that I had given more space to the distinct examination of the question so much controverted, wherein consists the efficaciousness of grace, and which the systems of different schools attribute to a physical premotion, to congruous grace, to concomitant grace, to a delectation which overcomes by reason of a moral action, or to a delectation which overcomes by reason of its superiority in degree. But for this, such a book as this, which I deliberately intended should be small and easily readable, would not have been enough. To explore this vast sea, many volumes would have been required. But this work has been sufficiently performed by others, and, moreover, it was beside my purpose. Still, I wished to establish the point treated of in my second part for the honor of God's providence and goodness, and to be of assistance to sinners, to prevent them from giving themselves up to despair because they think themselves deprived of grace; and also to take from them all excuse if they say that they have not strength to resist the assaults of the senses and of hell. I have shown them that of those who are lost, no one is damned for the original sin of Adam but solely for his own fault, because God refuses to no one the grace of prayer, whereby we may obtain his assistance to overcome every concupiscence and every temptation.

For the rest, my principal intention was to recommend to all men the use of prayer as the most powerful and necessary means of grace, in order that all men should more diligently and earnestly attend to it if they wish to be saved; for many poor souls lose God's grace, and continue to live in sin, and are finally damned, for this very reason: that they do not pray nor have recourse to God for assistance. The worst of the matter is (I cannot help saying so) that so few preachers and so few confessors have any definite purpose of indoctrinating their hearers and penitents with the use of prayer, without which it is impossible to observe the law of God, and to obtain perseverance in his grace.

Having observed that so many passages, both of the Old and the New Testament, assert the absolute necessity of prayer, I have made it a rule to introduce into all the missions, as given by our Congregation for several years, a sermon on prayer; and I say, and repeat, and will keep repeating as long as I live, that our whole salvation depends on prayer; and, therefore that all writers in their books, all preachers in their sermons, all confessors in their instructions to their penitents, should not inculcate anything more strongly than continual prayer. They should always admonish, exclaim, and continually repeat: "Pray, pray, never cease to pray; for if you pray, your salvation will be secure; but if you leave off praying, your damnation will be certain." All preachers and directors ought to do this because, according to the opinion of every Catholic school, there is no doubt of this truth that he who prays obtains grace and is saved; but those who practice it are too few, and this is the reason why so few are saved.

DEVOUT PRACTICES

I. Prayer to obtain final perseverance

Eternal Father, I humbly adore and thank you for having created me and for having redeemed me by means of Jesus Christ. I thank you for having made me a Christian by giving me the true faith and by adopting me for your child in holy baptism. I thank you for having given me time for repentance after my many sins and for having, as I hope, pardoned all my offenses against you. I renew my sorrow for them because I have displeased you. O Infinite Goodness! I thank you also for having preserved me from falling again as often as I should have done if you had not held me up and saved me. But my enemies do not cease to fight against me, nor will they until death, that they may again have me for their slave; if you do not keep and help me continually by your assistance, I shall be wretched enough to lose your grace anew. I therefore pray you, for the love of Jesus Christ, to grant me holy perseverance till death. Your Son Jesus has promised that you will grant us whatever we ask for in his name; by the merits, then, of Jesus Christ, I beg of you for myself, and for all those who are in your grace, the grace of never more being separated from your love, but that we may always love you in this life and in the next.

Mary, Mother of God, pray to Jesus for me.

II. Prayer to Jesus Christ to obtain his Holy Love

My crucified Love, my dear Jesus! I believe in you and confess you to be the true Son of God and my Savior. I adore you from the abyss of my own nothingness, and I thank you for the death you did suffer for me, that I might obtain the life of divine grace. My beloved Redeemer, to you I owe all my salvation. Through you I have hitherto escaped hell; through you have I received the pardon of my sins. But I am so ungrateful that, instead of loving you, I have repeated my offenses against you. I deserve to be condemned, so as not to be able to love you any more. But no, my Jesus, punish me in any other way, but not in this. If I have not loved you in time past, I love you now; and I desire nothing but to love you with all my heart. But without your help I can do nothing. Since you command me to love you, give me also the strength to fulfill this, your sweet and loving precept. You have promised to grant all that we ask of you: "You shall ask whatever you will, and it shall be done unto you" (John 15:7). Confiding, then, in this promise, my dear Jesus, I ask, first of all, pardon of all my sins; and I repent, above all things, because I have offended you, O Infinite Goodness! I ask for holy perseverance in your grace till my death. But, above all, I ask for the gift of your holy love. Ah, my Jesus, my Hope, my Love, my All, inflame me with that love which you came on earth to enkindle! For this end, make me always live in conformity with your holy will. Enlighten me, that I may understand more and more how worthy you are of our love, and that I may know the immense love you have borne me, especially in giving your life for me. Grant, then, that I may love you with all my heart, and may love you always, and never cease to beg of you the grace to love you in this life; that living always, and dying in your love, I may come one day to love you with all my strength in heaven, never to leave off loving you for all eternity.

Mother of beautiful love, my advocate and refuge, Mary, who are of all creatures the most beautiful, the most loving, and the most beloved of God, and whose only desire it is to see him loved! Ah, by the love you bear to Jesus Christ, pray for me, and obtain for me the grace to love him always, and with all my heart! This I ask and hope for from you. Amen.

III. Prayer to obtain confidence in the merits of Jesus Christ and in the intercession of Mary

Eternal Father, I thank you for myself, and on behalf of all mankind, for the great mercy that you have shown us in sending your Son to be made man and to die to obtain our salvation; I thank you for it, and I should wish to offer you in thanksgiving all that love which is due for such an inestimable benefit. By his merits our sins are pardoned, and your justice is satisfied for the punishment we had merited; by these merits you receive us miserable sinners into your grace, while we deserve nothing but hatred and chastisement: you receive men to reign in Paradise. Finally, you have bound yourself, in consideration of these merits, to grant all gifts and graces to those who ask for them in the name of Jesus Christ.

I thank you also, O Infinite Goodness, that, in order to strengthen our confidence, besides giving us Jesus Christ as our Redeemer, you have also given us your beloved daughter Mary as our advocate; so that, with that heart full of mercy which you have given her, she may never cease to succor by her intercession any sinner who may have recourse to her; and this intercession is so powerful with you that you cannot deny her any grace which she asks of you.

Hence it is your will that we should have a great confidence in the merits of Jesus and in the intercession of Mary. But this confidence is your gift, and it is a great gift which you grant to those only who ask you for it. This confidence, then, in the blood of Jesus Christ and in the patronage of Mary, I beg of you, through the merits of Jesus and Mary. To you, also, my dear Redeemer, do I turn; it was to obtain for me this confidence in your merits that you did sacrifice your life on the cross for me, who was worthy only of punishment. Accomplish, then, the end for which you have died; enable me to hope for all things, through confidence in your Passion.

And you, O Mary, my Mother, and my hope after Jesus, obtain for me a firm confidence, first in the merits of Jesus your Son, and then in the intercession of your prayers, prayers which are all-powerful in gaining all they ask!

O my beloved Jesus! O sweet Mary! I trust in you. To you do I give my soul; you have loved it so much; have pity on it and save it.

IV. Prayer to obtain the grace of being constant in prayer

God of my soul, I hope in your goodness that you have pardoned all my offenses against you, and that I am now in a state of grace. I thank you for it with all my heart, and I hope to thank you for all eternity (Psalm 89:2). I know that I have fallen because I have not had recourse to you when I was tempted, to ask for holy perseverance. For the future, I firmly resolve to recommend myself always to you, and especially when I see myself in danger of again offending you. I will always fly to your mercy, invoking always the most holy names of Jesus and Mary, with full confidence that when I pray you will not fail to give me the strength which I have not of myself to resist my enemies. This I resolve and promise to do.

But of what use, O my God, will all these resolutions and promises be if you do not assist me with your grace to put them in practice—that is, to have recourse to you in all dangers? Ah, Eternal Father! Help me, for the love of Jesus Christ, and let me never omit recommending myself to you whenever I am tempted. I know that you do always help me when I have recourse to you; but my fear is that I should forget to recommend myself to you, and so my negligence will be the cause of my ruin, that is, the loss of your grace, the greatest evil that can happen to me. Ah, by the merits of Jesus Christ, give me grace to pray to you; but grant me such an abundant grace that I may always pray, and pray as I ought!

O my Mother Mary, whenever I have had recourse to you, you have obtained for me the help which has kept me from falling! Now I come to beg of you to obtain a still greater grace, namely, that of recommending myself always to your Son and to you in all my necessities. My Queen, you obtain all you desire from God by the love you bear to Jesus Christ; obtain for me now this grace which I beg of you, namely, to pray always, and never to cease praying till I die. Amen.

V. Prayer to be said every day, to obtain the graces necessary for salvation

Eternal Father, your Son has promised that you will grant us all the graces which we ask you for in his name. In the name, therefore, and by the merits of Jesus Christ, I ask the following graces for myself and for all mankind. And, first, I pray you to give me a lively faith in all that the holy Roman Church teaches me. Enlighten me also that I may know the vanity of the goods of this world and the immensity of the infinite good that you are; make me also see the deformity of the sins I have committed, that I may humble myself and detest them as I ought; and, on the other hand, show me how worthy you are by reason of your goodness that I should love you with all my heart. Make me know also the love you have borne me, that from this day forward I may try to be grateful for so much goodness. Secondly, give me a firm confidence in your mercy of receiving the pardon of my sins, holy perseverance, and, finally, the glory of paradise, through the merits of Jesus Christ and the intercession of Mary. Thirdly, give me a great love toward you, which shall detach me from the love of this world and of myself, so that I may love none other but you, and that I may neither do nor desire anything else but what is for your glory. Fourthly, I beg of you a perfect resignation to your will, in accepting with tranquility sorrows, infirmities, contempt, persecutions, aridity of spirit, loss of property, of esteem, of relatives, and every other cross which shall come to me from your hands. I offer myself entirely to you, that you may do with me and all that belongs to me what you please. Only give me light and strength to do your will; and especially at the hour of death help me to sacrifice my life to you with all the affection I am capable of, in union with the sacrifice which your Son Jesus Christ made of his life on the Cross on Calvary. Fifthly, I beg of you a great sorrow for my sins, which may make me grieve over them as long as I live, and weep for the insults I have offered you, the Sovereign Good, who are worthy of infinite love, and who have loved me so much. Sixthly, I pray you to give me the spirit of true humility and meekness, that I may accept with peace, and even with joy, all the contempt, ingratitude, and ill-treatment that I may receive. At the same time, I also pray you to give me perfect charity, which shall make me wish well to those who have done evil to me, and to do what good I can, at least by praying, for those who have in any way injured me. Seventhly, I beg of you to give me a love for the virtue of holy mortification, by which I may chastise my rebellious senses and cross my self-love; at the same time, I beg you to give me holy purity of body and the grace to resist all bad temptations by ever having recourse to you and your most holy Mother. Give me grace faithfully to obey my spiritual Father and all my Superiors in all things. Give me an upright intention, that in all I desire and do I may seek only your glory and to please you alone. Give me a great confidence in the Passion of Jesus Christ and in the intercession of Mary Immaculate. Give me a great love toward the most Adorable Sacrament of the Altar and a tender devotion and love to your holy Mother. Give me, I pray you, above all, holy perseverance and the grace always to pray for it, especially in time of temptation and at the hour of death.

Lastly, I recommend to you the holy souls of Purgatory, my relatives and benefactors; and in an especial manner I recommend to you all those who hate me or who have in any way offended me; I beg of you to render them good for the evil they have done or may wish to do me. Finally, I recommend to you all infidels, heretics, and all poor sinners; give them light and strength to deliver themselves from sin. O most loving God, make yourself known and loved by all, but especially by those who have been more ungrateful to you than others, so that by your goodness I may come one day to sing your mercies in paradise; for my hope is in the merits of your blood and in the patronage of Mary.

O Mary, Mother of God, pray to Jesus for me! So I hope; so may it be!

VI. Thoughts and ejaculations

God! Who knows what fate awaits me?
I shall be either eternally happy or eternally miserable.
Of what worth is all the world without God?
Let all be lost, but let not God be lost.
I love you, my Jesus, who died for me!
Would that I had died before I ever offended you!
I will rather die than lose God.
Jesus and Mary, you are my hope.
My God, help me, for the love of Jesus Christ!
My Jesus, you alone are sufficient for me!
Suffer me not to separate myself from you.
Give me your love, and then do with me what you please.

Whom shall I love, if I love not you, my God?

Eternal Father, help me, for the love of Jesus!

I believe in you, I hope in you, I love you!

Here I am, O Lord; do with me what you will!

When shall I see myself altogether yours, my God?

When shall I be able to say to you, "My God, I can lose you no more"?

Mary, my hope, have pity on me! Mother of God, pray to Jesus for me!

Lord, who am I that you should desire to be loved by me?

My God, I desire you alone, and nothing more.

I desire all that you will, and that alone.

Oh, that I might be annihilated for you, who was annihilated for me!

Toward you alone, my God, have I been ungrateful!

I have offended you enough; I will no longer displease you.

If I had died then, I could not have loved you any more.

Let me die before again offending you.

You have waited for me that I might love you. Yes, I will love you.

I consecrate the remainder of my life to you.

O my Jesus, draw me entirely to yourself!

You will not leave me; I will not leave you. I hope that we shall always love each another, O God of my soul!

My Jesus, make me all yours before I die!

Grant that when you shall come to judge me, I may see you with a benign countenance.

You have done more than enough to oblige me to love you. I love you, I love you!

Deign to accept the love of a sinner who has so often offended you.

You have given yourself all to me; I give myself all to you.

I desire to love you exceedingly in this life, that I may love you exceedingly in the next.

Teach me to know your great goodness, that I may love you very much.

You love those who love you. I love you; love me also.

Give me the love you requires of me.

I rejoice that you are infinitely happy.

Oh, that I had always loved you, and had died before I had offended you.

Grant that I may overcome all things to please you.

I give you my whole will; dispose of me as you please.

My pleasure is to please you, O Infinite Goodness!

I hope to love you for all eternity, O eternal God!

You are omnipotent; make me a saint.

You sought me while I was flying from you; you will not drive me away now that I seek after you.

I thank you for giving me time to love you. I thank you and love you!

Let me give myself entirely to you this day.

Punish me in anyway, but do not deprive me of the power of loving you.

I will love you, my God, without reserve.

I accept all sufferings and all contempt, provided I may love you.

I desire to die for you, who died for me.

I wish that all could love you, who died for me.

I wish that all could love you as you merit.

I wish to do everything that I know to be your pleasure.

I care more to please you than for all the pleasures of the world.

O holy will of God, you are my love!

O Mary, draw me entirely to God!

O my Mother, make me always have recourse to you; it is for you to make me a saint; this is my hope.

HYMN

INVOCATION OF THE BLESSED VIRGIN
IN TIME OF TEMPTATION

Haste, my Mother, run to help me;
Mother, haste, do not delay;
See from hell the envious serpent
Comes my troubling soul to slay.

Ah, his very look affrights me,
And his cruel rage I fear;
Whither fly, if he attacks me?
See him, see him coming near!

Lo, I I faint away with terror,
For if yet thou dost delay,
He will dart at me his venom;
Then, alas, I am his prey.

Cries and tears have nought availed me,
Spite of all, I see him there;
Saints I call till I am weary,
Still he stands with threat'ning air.

Now his mighty jaws are open,
And his forkèd tongue I see;
Ah, he coils to spring upon me,
Mother! Hasten, make him flee.

Prayer

Mary! Yes, the name of Mary
Strikes with dread my cruel foe,
Straight he flees, as from the sunbeam
Swiftly melts the winter's snow.

Now he's gone, but do thou ever
Stay beside me, Mother dear;
Then the hellish fiend to tempt me
Nevermore will venture near.

Printed in Great Britain
by Amazon